Louisa May Alcott

Kitty's Class-Day; Aunt Kipp; Psyche's Art

Louisa May Alcott

Kitty's Class-Day; Aunt Kipp; Psyche's Art

ISBN/EAN: 9783337176297

Printed in Europe, USA, Canada, Australia, Japan

Cover: Foto ©ninafisch / pixelio.de

More available books at **www.hansebooks.com**

KITTY'S CLASS-DAY.
"A Stitch in time, saves nine."

AUNT KIPP.
"Children and Fools speak the truth."

PSYCHE'S ART
"Handsome is, that handsome does."

By LOUISA M. ALCOTT.

Six Illustrations, by Augustus Hoppin.

LORING, Publisher,
No. 369 Washington Street,
BOSTON.

Entered according to Act of Congress, in the year 1868, by

A. K. LORING,

in the Clerk's office of the District Court for the District of Massachusetts.

KITTY'S CLASS-DAY.

"A stitch in time saves nine."

"O Pris, Pris, I'm really going! Here's the invitation — rough paper — Chapel — spreads — Lyceum Hall — everything splendid; and Jack to take care of me!"

As Kitty burst into the room and performed a rapturous *pas seul*, waving the cards over her head, sister Priscilla looked up from her work with a smile of satisfaction on her quiet face.

"Who invites you, dear?"

"Why, Jack, of course, — dear old cousin Jack. Nobody else ever thinks of me, or cares whether I have a bit of pleasure now and then.

Isn't he kind? Mayn't I go? and, O Pris, what *shall* I wear?"

Kitty paused suddenly, as if the last all-important question had a solemnizing effect upon both mind and body.

"Why, your white muslin, silk sacque, and new hat, of course," began Pris, with an air of surprise. But Kitty broke in impetuously:—

"I'll never wear that old muslin again; it's full of darns, up to my knees, and all out of fashion. So is my sacque; and as for my hat, though it does well enough here, it would be absurd for Class Day."

"You don't expect an entirely new suit for this occasion,— do you?" asked Pris, anxiously.

"Yes, I do, and I'll tell you how I mean to get it. I've planned everything; for, though I hardly dreamed of going, I amused myself by thinking how I could manage if I *did* get invited."

"Let us hear." And Pris took up her work with an air of resignation.

"First, my dress," began Kitty, perching herself on the arm of the sofa, and entering into the subject with enthusiasm. "I've got the ten dollars grandpa sent me, and with eight of it I'm going to buy Lizzie King's organdie muslin. She got it in Paris; but her aunt providentially — no, unfortunately — died; so she can't wear it, and wants to get rid of it. She is bigger than I am, you know; so there is enough for a little mantle or sacque, for it isn't made up. The skirt is cut off and gored lovely, with a splendid train —"

"My dear, you don't mean you are going to wear one of those absurd new-fashioned dresses?" exclaimed Pris, lifting her hands and eyes.

"I do! Nothing would induce me to go to Class Day without a train. It's been the desire of my heart to have one, and now I *will*, if I never have another gown to my back!" returned Kitty, with immense decision.

Pris shook her head, and said, "Go on!" as if prepared for any extravagance after that.

"We can make it ourselves," continued Kitty, "and trim it with the same. It's white, with blue stripes, and daisies in the stripes; the loveliest thing you ever saw, and can't be got here. So simple, yet distingué, I know you'll like it. Next, my bonnet,"—here the solemnity of Kitty's face and manner was charming to behold. "I shall make it out of one of my new illusion undersleeves. I've never worn them; and the puffed part will be a plenty for a little fly-away bonnet of the latest style. I've got blue ribbons to tie it with, and have only to look up some daisies for the inside. With my extra two dollars I shall buy my gloves, and pay my fares — and there I am, all complete."

She looked so happy, so pretty, and full of girlish satisfaction, that sister Pris couldn't bear to disturb the little plan, much as she disapproved of it. They were poor, and every penny had to be counted. There were plenty of neighbors to gossip and criticise, and plenty of friends to make disagreeable remarks on any unusual extravagance. Pris saw things with the prudent eyes of thirty, but Kitty with the romantic eyes of seventeen; and the elder sister, in the kindness of her heart, had no wish to sadden life to those bright young eyes, or deny the child a harmless pleasure. She sewed thoughtfully for a minute, then looked up, saying, with the smile that always assured Kitty the day was won: —

"Get your things together, and we will see what can be done. But remember, dear, that it is both bad taste and bad economy for poor people to try to ape the rich."

"You're a perfect angel, Pris; so don't moralize. I'll run and get the dress, and we'll begin at once, for there's lots to do, and only two days to do it in." And Kitty skipped away, singing "Lauriger Horatius" at the top of her voice.

Priscilla soon found that the girl's head was completely turned by the advice and example of certain fashionable young neighbors. It was in vain for Pris to remonstrate and warn.

"Just this once let me do as others do, and thoroughly enjoy myself," pleaded Kitty; and Pris yielded, saying to herself, "She shall have her wish, and if she learns a lesson, neither time nor money will be lost."

So they snipped and sewed, and planned and pieced, going through all the alternations of despair and triumph, worry and satisfaction, which women undergo when a new suit is under way. Company kept coming, for news of Kitty's expedition had flown abroad, and her young friends must just run in to hear about it, and ask what she was going to wear; while Kitty was so glad and proud to tell, and show, and enjoy her little triumph that many half hours were wasted, and the second day found "lots" still to do.

The lovely muslin didn't hold out, and Kitty sacrificed the waist to the train, for a train she must have, or the whole thing would be an utter failure. A little sacque was eked out, however, and when the frills were on, it was "ravishing," as Kitty said, with a sigh of mingled delight and fatigue. The gored skirt was a fearful job, as any one who has ever plunged into the mysteries will testify; and before the facing even experienced Pris quailed.

The bonnet also was a trial, for when the lace was on, it was discovered that the ribbons didn't match the dress. Here was a catastrophe! Kitty frantically rummaged the house, the shops, the stores of her friends, and rummaged in vain. There was no time to send to the city, and despair was about to fall on Kitty, when Pris rescued her by quietly making one of the small sacrifices which were easy to her because her life was spent for others. Some one suggested a strip of blue illusion, — and that could be got; but, alas! Kitty had no money, for the gloves were already bought. Pris heard the lamentations, and, giving up fresh ribbons for herself, pulled her sister out of a slough of despond with two yards of "heavenly tulle."

"Now the daisies; and oh, dear me, not one can I find in this poverty-stricken town," sighed Kitty, prinking at the glass, and frequently hoping that nothing would happen to her complexion over night.

"I see plenty just like those on your dress,"

answered Pris, nodding toward the meadow full of young white-weed.

"Pris, you're a treasure! I'll wear real ones; they keep well, I know, and are so common I can refresh my bonnet anywhere. It's a splendid idea."

Away rushed Kitty, to return with an apron full of American daisies. A pretty cluster was soon fastened just over the left-hand frizzle of bright hair, and the little bonnet was complete.

"Now, Pris, tell me how I look," cried Kitty, as she swept into the room late that afternoon in full gala costume.

It would have been impossible for the primmest, the sourest, or the most sensible creature in the world to say that it wasn't a pretty sight. The long train, the big chignon, the apology for a bonnet, were all ridiculous, — no one could deny that, — but youth, beauty, and a happy heart made even those absurdities charming.

The erect young figure gave an air to the crisp folds of the delicate dress; the bright eyes and fresh cheeks under the lace rosette made one forget its size; and the rippling brown hair won admiration in spite of the ugly bunch which disfigured the girl's head. The little jacket set "divinely," the new gloves were as immaculate as white kids could be, and, to crown all, Lizzie King, in a burst of generosity, lent Kitty the blue and white Paris sunshade which she couldn't use herself.

"Now I could die content; I'm perfect in all respects, and I know Jack won't be ashamed of me. I really owe it to him to look my best, you know, and that's why I'm so particular," said Kitty, in an apologetic tone, as she began to lay away her finery.

"I hope you will enjoy every minute of the time, deary. Don't forget to finish running up the facing; I've basted it carefully, and would do it if my head didn't ache so I really can't hold it up any longer," answered Pris, who had worked like a disinterested bee, while Kitty had flown about like a distracted butterfly.

"Go and lie down, you dear, kind soul, and don't think of my nonsense again," said Kitty, feeling remorseful till Pris was comfortably asleep, when she went to her room and revelled in her finery till bedtime. So absorbed was she in learning to manage her train gracefully that she forgot the facing till very late. Then, being worn out with work and worry, she did what girls are too apt to do, stuck a pin here and there, and, trusting to Priscilla's careful bastings, left it as it was, retiring to dream of a certain Horace Fletcher, whose aristocratic elegance had made a deep impression upon her during the few evenings she had seen him.

Nothing could have been lovelier than the morning, and few hearts happier than Kitty's as she arrayed herself with the utmost care, and waited in solemn state for the carriage; for muslin trains and dewy roads were incompatible, and one luxury brought another.

"My goodness, where did she get that stylish suit?" whispered Miss Smith to Miss Jones, as Kitty floated into the station with all sail set, finding it impossible to resist the temptation to "crush" certain young ladies who had snubbed her in times past, which snubs had rankled, and were now avenged.

"I looked everywhere for a muslin for to-day and couldn't find any I liked, so I was forced to wear my mauve silk," observed Miss Smith, complacently settling the silvery folds of her dress.

"It's very pretty, but one ruins a silk at Class Day, you know. I thought this organdie would be more comfortable and appropriate this warm day. A friend brought it from Paris, and it's like one the Princess of Wales wore at the great flower-show this year," returned Kitty, with the air of a young lady who had all her dresses from Paris, and was intimately acquainted with the royal family.

"Those girls" were entirely extinguished by this stroke, and hadn't a word to say for themselves, while Kitty casually mentioned Horace Fletcher, Lyceum Hall, and cousin Jack, for *they* had only a little Freshman brother to boast of, and were *not* going to Lyceum Hall.

As she stepped out of the cars at Cambridge, Jack opened his honest blue eyes and indulged in a low whistle of astonishment; for if there was anything he especially hated it was "gowns with tails to 'em, knobs, and pancakes," as he irreverently called the last fashionable feminine adornments. He was very fond of Kitty, and prided himself on being able to show his friends a girl who was "stunningly pretty," and yet not dressed to death.

"She has made a regular guy of herself; I won't tell her so, and the dear little soul shall have a jolly time in spite of her fuss and feathers. But I do wish she had let her hair alone, and worn that killing hat of hers."

As this thought passed through Jack's mind he smiled and bowed, and made his way among the crowd, whispering as he drew his cousin's arm through his own: —

"I say, Kitty, you're got up regardless, aren't you? I'm so glad you came; we'll have a rousing good time, and you shall go in for all the fun."

"Oh, thank you, Jack! Do I look nice, really? I tried to be a credit to you and Pris, and I did have such a job of it. I'll make you shout over it some time. A carriage for me? Bless us, how fine we are!" and Kitty stepped in, feeling that only one thing more was needed to make her cup overflow. That one thing was speedily vouchsafed, for before her skirts were smoothly settled, Jack called out, in his hearty way : —

" How are you, Fletcher? If you are bound for Chapel I'll take you up."

" Thanks; good-morning, Miss Heath."

It was all done in an instant, and the next thing Kitty knew she was rolling away with the elegant Horace sitting opposite. How little it takes to make a young girl happy! A pretty dress, sunshine, and somebody opposite, and they are blest. Kitty's face glowed and dimpled with pleasure as she glanced about her, especially when *she*, sitting in state with two gentlemen all to herself, passed "those girls" walking in the dust with a beardless boy; she felt that she could forgive past slights, and did so with a magnanimous smile and bow.

Both Jack and Fletcher had graduated the year before, but still took an interest in their old haunts, and patronized the fellows who were not yet through the mill, at least the Seniors and Juniors; of Sophs and Freshs they were sublimely unconscious. Greeted by slaps on the shoulder, and hearty "How are you, old fellows?" they piloted Kitty to a seat in the Chapel. An excellent place, but the girl's satisfaction was marred by Fletcher's desertion, and she wouldn't see anything attractive about the dashing young lady in the pink bonnet to whom he devoted himself, "because she was a stranger," Kitty said.

Everybody knows what goes on in the Chapel, after the fight and scramble are over. The rustle and buzz, the music, the oratory and the poem, during which the men cheer and the girls simper, the professors yawn, and the poet's friends pronounce him a second Longfellow. Then the closing flourishes, the grand crush, and general scattering.

Then the fun really begins, as far as the young folks are concerned. *They* don't mind swarming up and down stairs in a solid phalanx; they can enjoy half-a-dozen courses of salad, ice, and strawberries, with stout gentlemen crushing their feet, anxious mammas sticking sharp elbows into their sides, and absent-minded tutors walking over them; they can flirt vigorously in a torrid atmosphere of dinner, dust, and din; can smile with hot coffee running down their backs, small avalanches of ice-cream descending upon their best bonnets, the sandwiches, butter-side down, reposing on their delicate silks. They know that it is a costly rapture, but they carefully refrain from thinking of the morrow, and energetically illustrate the Yankee maxim which bids us enjoy ourselves in our early bloom.

Kitty did have a rousing good time; for Jack was devoted, taking her everywhere, showing her everything, feeding and fanning her, and festooning her train with untiring patience. How many forcible expressions he mentally indulged in as he walked on that unlucky train we will not record; he smiled and skipped and talked of treading on flowers in a way that would have charmed Kitty, if some one else had not been hovering about "The Daisy," as Fletcher called her.

After he returned, she neglected Jack, who took it coolly, and was never in the way unless she wanted him. For the first time in her life, Kitty deliberately flirted. The little coquetries, which are as natural to a gay young girl as her laughter, were all in full play, and had she gone no farther no harm would have been done. But, excited by the example of those about her, Kitty tried to enact the fashionable young lady, and, like most novices, she overdid the part. Quite forgetting her cousin, she rolled her eyes, tossed her head, twirled her fan, gave affected little shrieks at college jokes, and talked college slang in a way that convulsed Fletcher, who enjoyed the fun immensely.

Jack saw it all, shook his head, and said nothing; but his face grew rather sober as he watched Kitty, flushed, dishevelled, and breathless, whirling round Lyceum Hall on the arm of Fletcher, who danced divinely, as all the girls agreed. Jack had proposed going, but Kitty had frowned, so he fell back, leaving her to listen and laugh, blush and shrink a little at her partner's flowery compliments and admiring glances.

"If she stands that long, she's not the girl I took her for," thought Jack, beginning to lose patience. "She don't look like my little Kitty, and somehow I don't feel half so fond and proud of her as usual. I know one thing, *my* daughters shall never be seen knocking about in that style."

As if the thought suggested the act, Jack suddenly assumed an air of paternal authority, and, arresting his cousin as she was about to begin again, he said, in a tone she had never heard before: —

"I promised Pris to take care of you, so I shall carry you off to rest, and put yourself to rights after this game of romps. I advise you to do the same, Fletcher, or give your friend in the pink bonnet a turn."

Kitty took Jack's arm pettishly, but glanced over her shoulder with such an inviting smile that Fletcher followed, feeling very much like a top, in danger of tumbling down the instant he stopped spinning. As she came out Kitty's face cleared, and, assuming her sprightliest air, she spread her plumage and prepared to descend with effect, for a party of uninvited *peris* stood at the gate of this Paradise casting longing glances at the forbidden splendors within. Slowly, that all might see her, Kitty sailed down, with Horace, the debonnair, in her wake, and was just thinking to herself, "Those girls won't get over this very soon, I fancy," when all in one moment she heard Fletcher exclaim, wrathfully, "Hang the flounces!" she saw a very glossy black beaver come skipping down the steps, felt a violent twitch backward, and, to save herself from a fall, sat down on the lower step with most undignified haste.

It was impossible for the bystanders to help laughing, for there was Fletcher hopping wildly about, with one foot nicely caught in a muslin loop, and there sat Kitty, longing to run away and hide herself, yet perfectly helpless, while every one tittered. Miss Jones and Miss Smith laughed shrilly, and the despised little Freshman completed her mortification, by a feeble joke about Kitty Heath's new man-trap. It was only an instant, but it seemed an hour, before Fletcher freed her, and, snatching up the dusty beaver, left her with a flushed countenance and an abrupt bow.

If it hadn't been for Jack, Kitty would have burst into tears then and there, so terrible was the sense of humiliation which oppressed her. For his sake she controlled herself, and, bundling up her torn train, set her teeth, stared straight before her, and let him lead her in dead silence to a friend's room near by. There he locked the door and began to comfort her by making light of the little mishap. But Kitty cried so tragically, that he was at his wit's end, till the ludicrous side of the affair struck her, and she began to laugh hysterically. With a vague idea that vigorous treatment was best for that feminine ailment, Jack was about to empty the contents of an ice-pitcher over her, when she arrested him by exclaiming, incoherently: —

"Oh, don't! — it was so funny! — how can you laugh, you cruel boy? — I'm disgraced forever — take me home to Pris, oh, take me home to Pris!"

"I will, my dear, I will; but first let me right you up a bit; you look as if you had been hazed, upon my life you do;" and Jack laughed in spite of himself at the wretched little object before him, for dust, dancing, and the downfall produced a ruinous spectacle.

That broke Kitty's heart; and, spreading her hands before her face, she was about to cry again, when the sad sight which met her eyes dispelled the gathering tears. The new gloves were both split up the middle and very dirty with clutching at the steps as she went down.

"Never mind, you can wash 'em," said Jack, soothingly.

"It's awful! I paid a dollar and a half for 'em, and they can't be washed," groaned Kitty.

"Oh, hang the gloves! I meant your hands," cried Jack, trying to keep sober.

"No matter for my hands; I mourn my gloves. But I won't cry any more, for my head aches now so I can hardly see." And Kitty threw off her bonnet, as if even that airy trifle hurt her.

Seeing how pale she looked, Jack tenderly suggested a rest on the old sofa, and a wet handkerchief on her hot forehead, while he got the good landlady to send her up a cup of tea. As Kitty rose to comply she glanced at her dress, and, clasping her hands, exclaimed, tragically:—

"The facing, the fatal facing! That made all the mischief; for if I'd sewed it last night it wouldn't have ripped to-day; if it hadn't ripped Fletcher wouldn't have got his foot in it, I shouldn't have made an object of myself, he wouldn't have gone off in a rage, and — who knows what might have happened?"

"Bless the what's-its-name if it has settled him," cried Jack. "He is a contemptible fellow not to stay and help you out of the scrape he got you into. Follow his lead and don't trouble yourself about him."

"Well, he *was* rather absurd to-day, I allow; but he *has* got handsome eyes and hands, and he *does* dance like an angel," sighed Kitty, as she pinned up the treacherous loop which had brought destruction to her little castle in the air.

"Handsome eyes, white hands, and angelic feet don't make a man. Wait till you can do better, Kit."

With an odd, grave look, that rather startled Kitty, Jack vanished, to return presently with a comfortable cup of tea and a motherly old lady to help repair damages and soothe her by the foolish little purrings and pattings so grateful to female nerves after a flurry.

"I'll come back and take you out to see the dance round the tree when you've had a bit of a rest," said Jack, vibrating between door and sofa as if it wasn't easy to get away.

"Oh, I couldn't," cried Kitty, with a shudder at the bare idea of meeting any one. "I can't be seen again to-night; let me stay here till my train goes."

"I thought it had gone already," said Jack, with an irrepressible twinkle of the eye that glanced at the draggled dress sweeping the floor.

"How *can* you joke about it!" and the girl's reproachful eyes filled with tears of shame. "I know I've been a fool, Jack; but I've had my punishment, and I don't need any more.

To feel that you despise me is worse than all the rest."

She ended with a little sob, and turned her face away to hide the trembling of her lips. At that, Jack flushed up, his eyes shone, and he stooped suddenly as if to make some impetuous reply. But, remembering the old lady (who, by-the-by, was discreetly looking out of the window), he put his hands in his pockets and strolled out of the room.

"I've lost them both by this day's folly," thought Kitty, as Mrs. Bliss departed with the teacup. "I don't care for Fletcher, for I dare say he didn't mean half he said, and I was only flattered because he is rich and handsome and the girls glorify him. But I shall miss Jack, for I've known and loved him all my life. How good he's been to me to-day! so patient, careful, and kind, though he must have been ashamed of me! I know he didn't like my dress; but he never said a word, and stood by me through everything. Oh, I wish I'd minded Pris! then he would have respected me, at least. I wonder if he ever will again?"

Following a sudden impulse, Kitty sprang up, locked the door, and then proceeded to destroy all her little vanities as far as possible. She smoothed out her crimps with a wet and ruthless hand; fastened up her pretty hair in the simple way Jack liked; gave her once-cherished bonnet a spiteful shake, as she put it on, and utterly extinguished it with a big blue veil. She looped up her dress, leaving no vestige of the now hateful train, and did herself up uncompromisingly in the Quakerish gray shawl Pris had insisted on her taking for the evening. Then she surveyed herself with pensive satisfaction, saying, in the tone of one bent on resolutely mortifying the flesh:—

"Neat, but not gaudy; I'm a fright, but I

deserve it, and it's better than being a peacock."

Kitty had time to feel a little friendless and forlorn, sitting there alone as twilight fell, and amused herself by wondering if Fletcher would come to inquire about her, or show any further interest in her; yet when the sound of a manly tramp approached, she trembled lest it should be the victim of the fatal facing. The door opened, and with a sigh of relief she saw Jack come in, bearing a pair of new gloves in one hand and a great bouquet of June roses in the other.

"How good of you to bring me these! They are more refreshing than oceans of tea. You know what I like, Jack; thank you very much," cried Kitty, sniffing at her roses with grateful rapture.

"And you know what I like," returned Jack,

with an approving glance at the altered figure before him.

"I'll never do so any more," murmured Kitty, wondering why she felt bashful all of a sudden, when it was only cousin Jack.

"Now put on your gloves, dear, and come out and hear the music; your train don't go for two hours yet, and you mustn't mope here all that time," said Jack, offering his second gift.

"How did you know my size?" asked Kitty, putting on the gloves in a great hurry; for though Jack had called her "dear" for years, the little word had a new sound to-night.

"I guessed, — no I didn't, I had the old ones with me; they are no good now, are they?" and, too honest to lie, Jack tried to speak carelessly, though he turned red in the dusk, well knowing that the dirty little gloves were folded away in his left breast-pocket at that identical moment.

"Oh, dear, no! these fit nicely. I'm ready, if you don't mind going with such a fright," said Kitty, forgetting her dread of seeing people in her desire to get away from that room, because for the first time in her life she wasn't at ease with Jack.

"I think I like the little gray moth better than the fine butterfly," returned Jack, who, in spite of his invitation, seemed to find "moping" rather pleasant.

"You are a rainy-day friend, and he isn't," said Kitty, softly, as she drew him away.

Jack's only answer was to lay his hand on the little white glove resting so confidingly on his arm, and, keeping it there, they roamed away into the summer twilight.

Something had happened to the evening and the place, for both seemed suddenly endowed with uncommon beauty and interest. The dingy old houses might have been fairy palaces, for anything they saw to the contrary; the dusty walks, the trampled grass, were regular Elysian fields to them, and the music was the music of the spheres, though they found themselves "Right in the middle of the boom, jing, jing." For both had made a little discovery, — no, not a little one, the greatest and sweetest man and woman can make. In the sharp twinge of jealousy which the sight of Kitty's flirtation with Fletcher gave him, and the delight he found in her after conduct, Jack discovered how much he loved her. In the shame, gratitude, and half-sweet, half-bitter emotion that filled her heart, Kitty felt that to her Jack would never be "only cousin Jack" any more. All the vanity, coquetry, selfishness, and ill-temper of the day seemed magnified to heinous sins, for now her only thought was, "seeing these faults, he *can't* care for me. Oh, I wish I was a better girl!"

She did not say "for his sake," but in the new humility, the ardent wish to be all that a woman should be, little Kitty proved how true her love was, and might have said with Portia: —

> "For myself alone, I would not be
> Ambitious in my wish; but, for you,
> I would be trebled twenty times myself;
> A thousand times more fair,
> Ten thousand times more rich."

All about them other pairs were wandering under the patriarchal elms, enjoying music, starlight, balmy winds, and all the luxuries of the season. If the band had played

> "Oh, there's nothing half so sweet in life
> As love's young dream —"

it is my private opinion that it would have suited the audience to a T. Being principally composed of elderly gentlemen with large families, they had not that fine sense of the fitness of things so charming to see, and tooted and banged away with waltzes and marches, quite regardless of the flocks of Romeos and Juliets philandering all about them.

Under cover of a popular medley, Kitty overheard Fletcher quizzing her for the amusement of Miss Pink-bonnet, who was evidently making up for lost time. It was feeble wit, but it put the finishing stroke to Kitty's vanity, and she wept a little weep in her blue tissue retreat, and clung to Jack, feeling that she had never valued him half enough. She hoped he didn't hear the gossip going on at the other side of the tree near which they stood; but he did, for his hand involuntarily doubled itself up into a very dangerous-looking fist, and he darted such fiery glances at the speaker, that, if the thing had been possible, Fletcher's ambrosia curls would have been scorched off his head.

"Never mind, and don't get angry, Jack. They are right about one thing, — the daisies in my bonnet *were* real, and I *couldn't* afford any others. I don't care much, only Pris worked so hard to get me ready I hate to have my things made fun of."

"He isn't worth a thrashing, so we'll let it pass this time," said Jack, irefully, yet privately resolving to have "a go" at Fletcher by and by.

"Why, Kitty, I thought the real daisies the prettiest things about your dress. Don't throw them away. I'll wear them just to show that noodle that I prefer nature to art;" and Jack gallantly stuck the faded posy in his button-hole, while Kitty treasured up the hint so kindly given for future use.

If a clock with great want of tact hadn't insisted on telling them that it was getting late, Kitty never would have got home, for both the young people felt inclined to loiter about arm in arm through the sweet summer night forever. Jack had meant to say something before she went, and was immensely surprised to find the chance lost for the present. He wanted to go home with her and free his mind; but a neighborly old gentleman having been engaged as escort, there would have been very little satisfaction in a travelling trio; so he gave it up. He was very silent as they walked to the station with Dr. Dodd trudging behind them. Kitty thought he was tired, perhaps glad to be rid of her, and meekly accepted her fate. But as the train approached, she gave his hand an impulsive squeeze, and said very gratefully: —

"Jack, I can't thank you enough for your kindness to your silly little cousin; but I never shall forget it, and if I ever can return it in any way, I will with all my heart."

Jack looked down at the young face almost

pathetic now with weariness, humility, and pain, yet very sweet, with that new shyness in the loving eyes, and, stooping suddenly, he kissed it, whispering in a tone that made the girl's heart flutter: —

"I'll tell you how you may return it with all your heart, by and by. Good-night, my Kitty."

"Have you had a good time, dear?" asked Pris, as her sister appeared an hour later.

"Don't I look as if I had?" and throwing off her wraps, Kitty revolved slowly before her that she might behold every portion of the wreck. "My gown is all dust, crumple, and rags, my bonnet perfectly limp and flat, and my gloves are ruined; I've broken Lizzie's parasol, made a spectacle of myself, and wasted money, time, and temper; yet my Class Day isn't a failure, for Jack is the dearest boy in the world, and I'm very, very happy!"

Pris looked at her a minute, then opened her arms without a word, and Kitty forgot all her little troubles in one great joy.

When Miss Smith and Miss Jones called a few days after to tell her that Mr. Fletcher was going abroad, the amiable creatures were entirely routed by finding Jack there in a most unmistakable situation. He blandly wished Horace "bon voyage," and regretted that he wouldn't be there to the wedding in October. Kitty devoted herself to blushing beautifully, and darning endless rents in a short daisy muslin skirt, "which I intend to wear a great deal, because Jack likes it, and so do I," she said, with a demure look at her lover, who laughed as if that was the best joke of the season.

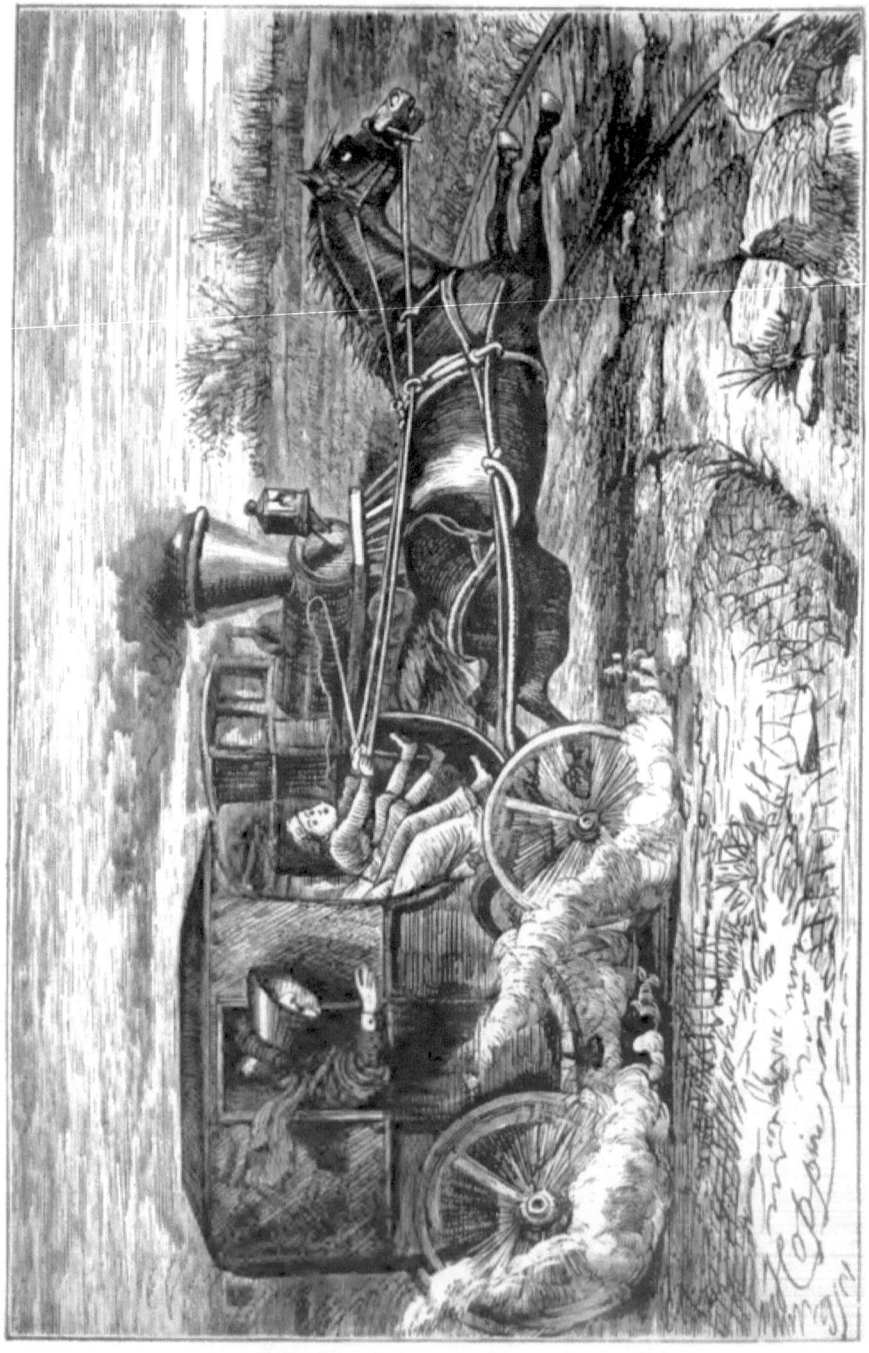

AUNT KIPP.

"Children and fools speak the truth."

I.

"What's that sigh for, Polly, dear?"

"I'm tired, mother, tired of working and waiting. If I'm ever going to have any fun, I want it *now* while I can enjoy it."

"You shouldn't wait another hour if I could have my way; but you know how helpless I am;" and poor Mrs. Snow sighed dolefully, as she glanced about the dingy room and pretty Mary turning her faded gown for the second time.

"If Aunt Kipp would give us the money she

is always talking about, instead of waiting till she dies, we should be *so* comfortable. She is a dreadful bore, for she lives in such terror of dropping dead with her heart-complaint that she don't take any pleasure in life herself or let any one else; so the sooner she goes, the better for all of us," said Polly, in a desperate tone; for things looked very black to her just then.

"My dear, don't say that," began her mother, mildly shocked; but a bluff little voice broke in with the forcible remark: —

"She's everlastingly tellin' me never to put off till to-morrer what can be done to-day; next time she comes I'll remind her of that, and ask her, if she is goin' to die, why she don't up and do it."

"Toady! you're a wicked, disrespectful boy; never let me hear you say such a thing again about your dear Aunt Kipp."

"She aint dear! You know we all hate her,

ma, and you are 'fraider of her'n you are of spiders, — so now."

The young personage, whose mellifluous name of Theodore had been corrupted into Toady, was a small boy of ten or eleven, apple-cheeked, round-eyed, and curly-headed; arrayed in well-worn, gray knickerbockers, profusely adorned with paint, glue, and shreds of cotton. Perched on a high stool, at an isolated table in a state of chaos, he was absorbed in making a boat, entirely oblivious of the racking tooth-ache which had been his excuse for staying from school. As cool, saucy, hard-handed, and soft-hearted a little specimen of young America was Toady as you would care to see — a tyrant at home, a rebel at school, a sworn foe to law, order, and Aunt Kipp. This young party was regarded as a reprobate by all but his mother, sister, and sister's sweetheart, Van Bahr Lamb. Having been, through much anguish of flesh and spirit, taught that lying was a deadly sin, Toady rushed to the other extreme, and bolted out the truth, the whole truth, and nothing but the truth, at all times and places, with a startling abruptness that brought wrath and dismay upon his friends and relatives.

"It's horrid to fib; you've whacked that into me and you can't rub it out, ma," he was wont to say with vivid recollection of the part tingling in the chubby portions of his frame.

"Mind your chips, Toady, and take care what you say to Aunt Kipp, or you'll be as poor as a little rat all the days of your life," said Polly, warningly.

"I don't want her old money, and I'll tell her so if she bothers me about it. I shall go into business with Van and take care of the whole lot; so don't you preach, Polly," returned Toady, with as much dignity as was compatible with a great dab of glue on the end of his snub nose.

"Ma, dear, did aunt say anything about coming this week?" asked Polly, after a pause of intense thought over a breadth with three darns, two spots, and a burn.

"Yes; she wrote that she was too feeble to come at present, as she had such dreadful palpitations she didn't dare stir from her room. So we are quite safe for the next week at least, and — bless my soul, there she is now!"

Mrs. Snow clasped her hands with a gesture of dismay, and sat as if transfixed by the spectacle of a ponderous lady, in an awe-inspiring bonnet, who came walking slowly down the street. Polly gave a groan, and pulled a bright ribbon from her hair. Toady muttered, "Oh, bother!" and vainly attempted to polish up his countenance with a fragmentary pocket-handkerchief.

"Nothing but salt-fish for dinner," wailed Mrs. Snow, as the shadow of the coming event fell upon her.

"Van will make a fool of himself, and ruin everything," sighed Polly, glancing at the ring on her finger.

"I know she'll kiss me; she never *will* let a fellow alone," growled Toady, scowling darkly.

The garden-gate clashed, dust flew from the door-mat, a heavy step echoed in the hall, an imperious voice called "Sophy!" and Aunt Kipp entered with a flourish of trumpets, for Toady blew a blast through his fingers which made the bows totter on her bonnet.

"My dear aunt, I'm very glad to see you," murmured Mrs. Snow, advancing with a smile of welcome; for though as weak as water-gruel, she was as kind-hearted a little woman as ever lived.

"My boots! what a whacker that was!" said Toady, *sotto voce*.

"We were just saying we were afraid you wouldn't" — began Mary, when a warning, "Mind your eye, Polly," caused her to stop short and busy herself with the new-comer's bag and umbrella.

"I changed my mind. Theodore, come and kiss me," answered Aunt Kipp, briefly.

"Yes'm," was the plaintive reply, and, closing his eyes, Toady awaited his fate with fortitude.

But the dreaded salute did not come, for Aunt Kipp exclaimed, in alarm: —

"Mercy on us! has the boy got the plague?"

"No'm, it's paint, and dirt, and glue, and it *won't* come off," said Toady, stroking his variegated countenance with grateful admiration for the stains that saved him.

"Go and wash this moment, sir. Thank Heaven *I've* got no boys," cried Aunt Kipp, as if boys were some virulent disease which she had narrowly escaped.

With a hasty peck at the lips of her two elder relatives, the old lady seated herself, and slowly removed the awful bonnet, which in shape and hue much resembled a hearse hung with black crape.

"I'm glad you are better," said Mary, reverently receiving the funereal head-gear.

"I'm *not* better," cut in Aunt Kipp. "I'm worse, much worse; my days are numbered; I stand on the brink of the tomb, and may drop at any moment."

Toady's face was a study, as he glanced up at the old lady's florid countenance, down at the floor, as if in search of the above-mentioned "brink," and looked unaffectedly anxious to see her drop. "Why don't you then?" was on his lips; but a frown from Polly restrained him, and he set himself down on the rug to contemplate the corpulent victim.

"Have a cup of tea, aunt?" said Mrs. Snow.

"I will."

"Lie down and rest a little," suggested Polly.

"I won't."

"Can we do anything for you?" said both.

"Take my things away, and have dinner early."

Both departed to perform these behests, and, leaning back in her chair, Aunt Kipp reposed.

"I say, what's a bore?" asked Toady, from the rug, where he sat rocking meditatively to and fro, holding on by his shoe-strings.

"It's a kind of a pig, very fierce, and folks are afraid of 'em," said Aunt Kipp, whose knowledge of Natural History was limited.

"Good for Polly! so you are!" sung out the boy, with the hearty child's laugh so pleasant to most ears.

"What do you mean, sir?" demanded the old lady, irefully poking at him with her umbrella.

"Why, Polly said you were a bore," explained Toady, with artless frankness. "You *are* fat, you know, and fierce sometimes, and folks are scared of you. Good, wasn't it?"

"Very! Mary is a nice, grateful, respectful, loving niece, and I shan't forget her, she may depend on that," and Aunt Kipp laughed grimly

"May she? well, that's jolly now. She was afraid you wouldn't give her the money; so I'll tell her it's all right;" and innocent Toady nodded approvingly.

"Oh, she expects some of my money, does she?"

"Course she does; aint you always saying you'll remember us in your will, 'cause pa was your favorite nephew, and all that? I'll tell you a secret, if you won't let Polly know I spoke first. You'll find it out to-night anyway. Van's so spooney on her, you'd see they were sweethearts in a minute."

"Sweethearts!" cried Aunt Kipp, turning red in the face.

"Yes'm. Van popped last week, and Polly's been going on like mad ever since. Ma likes it, and *I* like it, for I'm fond of Van, though I do call him Baa-baa, 'cause he looks like a sheep. We all like it, and we'd all hooray for it, if we wan't afraid of you. Ma and Polly I mean; of course we men don't mind, but we don't want a row. You won't make one, will you, now?"

Anything more expressive of brotherly goodwill, persuasive frankness, and a placid consciousness of having "fixed it," than Toady's dirty little face, it would be hard to find. Aunt Kipp eyed him so fiercely, that even before she spoke a dim suspicion that something was wrong began to dawn on his too confiding soul.

"*I* don't like it, and I'll put a stop to it. I won't have any ridiculous baa-baas in my family. If Mary counts on my money to begin housekeeping with, she'll find herself mistaken; for not one penny shall she have, married or single, and you may tell her so."

Toady was so taken aback by this explosion that he let go his shoe-strings, fell over with a crash, and lay flat, with shovel and tongs spread upon him like a pall. In rushed ma and Polly, to find the boy's spirits quite quenched, for once, and Aunt Kipp in a towering passion. It all came out in one overwhelming flood of words, and Toady fled from the storm to wander round the house, a prey to the deepest remorse. The meekness of that boy at dinner-time was so angelic that Mrs. Snow would have feared speedy translation for him, if she had not been very angry. Polly's red eyes, and Aunt Kipp's griffinesque expression of countenance, weighed upon his soul so heavily, that even roly-poly pudding failed to assuage his trouble, and, taking his mother into the china-closet, he anxiously inquired "if it was all up with Polly."

"I'm afraid so, for aunt vows she will make a new will to-morrow, and leave every penny to the Charitable Rag-bag Society," sighed Mrs. Snow.

"I didn't go to do it, ma; I truly didn't! I thought I'd just 'give her a hint,' as you say. She looked all serene, and laughed when I told her about being a bore, and I thought she liked it. If she was a man, I'd thrash her for making Polly cry;" and Toady shook his fist at Aunt Kipp's umbrella, which was an immense relief to his perturbed spirit.

"Bless the boy! I do believe he would!" cried Mrs. Snow, watching the little turkey-cock with maternal pride. "You can't do that; so just be careful and not make any more mischief, dear."

"I'll try, ma; but I'm always getting into scrapes with Aunt Kipp. She's worse'n measles, any day,—such an old aggrawater! I say, Van's coming this afternoon. Won't he make her clever again?"

"Oh, dear, no! He will probably make things ten times worse, he's so bashful and queer. I'm afraid our last chance is gone, deary, and we must grub along as we have done."

One sniff of emotion burst from Toady, and for a moment he laid his head in the knife-tray, overcome with disappointment and regret. But, scorning to yield to unmanly tears, he was soon himself again. Thrusting his beloved jack-knife, with three blades and a file, into Polly's hand, he whispered, brokenly:—

"Keep it forever'n' ever; I'm thundering sorry!" Then, feeling that the magnitude of this sacrifice atoned for everything, he went to watch for Van, — the forlorn hope to which he now clung.

II.

"Sophy, I'm surprised at your want of judgment. Do you really mean to let your girl marry this Lamb? Why, the man's a fool!" began Aunt Kipp, after dinner, by way of opening a pleasant conversation with her relatives.

"Dear me, aunt! how can you know that, when you never saw him?" mildly returned Mrs. Snow.

"I've heard of him, and that's enough for me. I've a deal of penetration in judging character, and I tell you Van Bahr Lamb is a fool."

The amiable old lady thought this would rouse Polly, against whom her anger still burned hotly. But Polly also possessed penetration; and, well knowing that contradiction would delight Aunt Kipp, she completely took the wind out of her sails, by coolly remarking: —

"I like fools."

"Bless my heart! what does the girl mean?" ejaculated Aunt Kipp.

"Just what I say. If Van is a fool, I prefer simpletons to wiseacres. I know he is shy and awkward, looks like a goose sometimes, and does absurd things now and then. But I also know that he has the kindest heart that ever was; is unselfish, faithful, and loving; that he took good care of his old parents till they died, and never thought of himself while they needed him. He loves me dearly; will wait for me a dozen years, if I say so, and work all his days to make me happy. He's a help and comfort to ma, a good friend to Toady, and I love, and respect, and am proud of him though he *is* a fool," cried Polly, heartily.

"And you insist on marrying him?" demanded Aunt Kipp.

"Yes, I do."

"Then I wish a carriage immediately," was the somewhat irrelevant reply.

"Why, aunt, you don't mean to go so soon?" cried Mrs. Snow, with a reproachful glance at the rebellious Polly.

"Far from it. I wish to see Judge Banks about altering my will," was the awful answer.

Polly's face fell; her mother gave a despairing sigh; Toady, who had hovered about the door, uttered a suppressed whistle of dismay; and Mrs. Kipp looked about her with vengeful satisfaction.

"Get the big carryall and old Bob, so the boy can drive, and all of you come; the trip will do you good."

It was like Aunt Kipp to invite her poor relations to go and "nip their own noses off," as she elegantly expressed it. It was a party of pleasure that just suited her, for all the fun was on her side. She grew affable at once; was quite pressing in her invitation; regretted that Sophy was too busy to go; praised Polly's hat; and professed herself quite satisfied with "that dear boy" for a driver. The "dear boy" distorted his young countenance frightfully behind her back, but found a balm for every wound in the delight of being commander of the expedition.

The big carryall appeared, and, with much creaking and swaying, Mrs. Kipp was got into the back seat, where the big bonnet gloomed like a thunder-cloud. Polly, in a high state of indignation, which only made her look ten times prettier, sat in front with Toady, who was a sight for gods and men as he drove off with his short legs planted against the boot, his elbows squared, and the big whip scientifically cracking now and then. Away they went, leaving poor ma to bewail herself dismally after she had smiled and nodded them out of sight.

"Don't go over any bridges or railroad crossings or by any saw-mills," said the old lady, as if the town could be suddenly remodelled to suit her taste.

"Yes'm," returned Toady, with a crack which would have done honor to a French postilion.

It was a fine day, and the young people would have enjoyed the ride in spite of the breakers ahead, if Aunt Kipp hadn't entertained the girl with a glowing account of the splendors of her own wedding, and aggravated the boy by frequent pokes and directions in the art of driving, of which she was, of course, profoundly ignorant. Polly couldn't restrain a tear or two, in thinking of her own poor little prospects, and Toady was goaded to desperation.

"I'll give her a regular shaking up; it'll make her hold her tongue and do her good," he said to himself, as a stony hill sloped temptingly before him.

A sly chuck, and some mysterious manœuvre with the reins, and Bob started off at a brisk trot, as if he objected to the old lady as much as her mischievous little nevvy.

"Hold him in! Keep a taut rein! Lord 'a mercy, he's running away!" shrieked Aunt Kipp, or tried to shriek, for the bouncing and bumping jerked the words out of her mouth with ludicrous incoherency.

"I am holding him, but he *will* go," said Toady, with a wicked triumph in his eye as he glanced back at Polly.

The next minute the words were quite true; for, as he spoke, two or three distracted hens flew squalling over the wall and scattered about under, over, and before the horse, as only distracted hens could do. It was too much for Bob's nerves; and, taking matters into his own hands, or feet, rather, he broke into a run, and rattled the old lady's bones over the stones with a velocity which left her speechless.

Polly laughed, and Toady chuckled, as they caught glimpses of the awful bonnet vibrating wildly in the background, and felt the frantic clutchings of the old lady's hands. But both grew sober as a shrill car-whistle sounded not far off; and Bob, as if possessed by an evil spirit, turned suddenly into the cross-road that led to the railroad-crossing.

"That will do, Toady; now pull up, for we can't get over in time," said Polly, glancing anxiously toward the rapidly approaching puffs of white smoke.

"I can't, Polly, — I really can't," cried the boy, tugging with all his might, and beginning to look scared.

Polly lent her aid; but Bob scarcely seemed to feel it, for he had been a racer once, and when his blood was up he was hard to handle. His own good sense might have checked him, if Aunt Kipp hadn't unfortunately recovered her voice at this crisis, and uttered a succession of the shrillest screams that ever saluted mortal ears. With a snort and a bound Bob dashed straight on toward the crossing, as the train appeared round the bend.

"Let me out! Let me out! Jump! Jump!" shrieked Aunt Kipp, thrusting her head out of the window, where it stuck, while she fumbled madly for the door-handle.

"O Toady, save us! save us!" gasped Polly, losing her presence of mind, and dropping the reins to cling to her brother, with a woman's instinctive faith in the stronger sex.

But Toady held on manfully, though his arms were nearly pulled off, for "Never say die," was his motto, and the plucky little lad wouldn't show fear before the women.

"Don't howl; we'll do it! Hi, Bob!" and with a savage slash of the whip, an exciting cry, a terrible reeling and rattling, they *did* do it; for Bob cleared the track at a breakneck pace, just in time for the train to sweep swiftly by behind them.

Aunt Kipp dropped in a heap, leaving the big bonnet firmly fixed in the window. Polly looked up at her brother, with a look which he never forgot; and Toady tried to say, stoutly, "It's all right!" with lips that were white and dry in spite of himself.

"We shall smash up at the bridge," he muttered, as they tore through the town, where every one obligingly shouted, waved their hats, and danced about on the sidewalks, doing nothing but add to Bob's fright and the party's danger. But Toady was wrong,—they didn't smash up at the bridge; for, before they reached the perilous spot, one man had the sense to fly straight at the horse's head and hold on like grim death till the momentary check enabled others to lend a hand.

The moment they were safe, Polly, like a regular heroine, threw herself into the arms of her dishevelled preserver, who of course was Van, and would have refreshed herself with hysterics if the sight of Toady hadn't steadied her. The boy sat as stiff and rigid as a wooden figure till they took the reins from him; then all the strength seemed to go out of him, and he leaned against his sister, as white and trembling as she, whispering with an irrepressible sob:—

"O Polly, wasn't it horrid? Tell ma I stood by you like a man. Do tell her that!"

If any one had had time or heart to laugh, they certainly would have done it when, after much groping, heaving, and hoisting, Mrs. Kipp was extricated and restored to consciousness; for a more ludicrously deplorable spectacle was seldom seen. Quite unhurt, though much shaken, the old lady insisted on believing herself to be dying, and kept the town in a ferment till three doctors had pronounced her perfectly well able to go home. Then the perversity of her nature induced her to comply, that she might have the satisfaction of dying on the way, and proving herself in the right.

Unfortunately she didn't expire, but, having safely arrived, went to bed in high dudgeon, and led Polly and her mother a sad life of it for two weary days. Having heard of Toady's gallant behavior, she solemnly ordered him up to receive her blessing. But the sight of Aunt Kipp's rubicund visage, surrounded by the rampantly stiff frills of an immense nightcap, caused the irreverent boy to explode with laughter in his handkerchief, and to be hustled away by his mother before Aunt Kipp discovered the true cause of his convulsed appearance.

"Ah! poor dear, his feelings are too much for him. He sees my doom in my face, and is overcome by what you refuse to believe. I shan't forget that boy's devotion. Now leave me to the meditations befitting these solemn hours."

Mrs. Snow retired, and Aunt Kipp tried to sleep; but the murmur of voices and the sound of stifled laughter in the next room disturbed her repose.

"They are rejoicing over my approaching end, knowing that I haven't changed my will. Mercenary creatures, don't exult too soon! there's time yet," she muttered; and presently, unable to control her curiosity, she crept out of bed to listen and peep through the key-hole.

Van Bahr Lamb did look like a sheep. He had a blond curly head, a long face, pale, mild eyes, a plaintive voice, and a general expression of innocent timidity strongly suggestive of animated mutton. But Baa-baa was a "trump," as Toady emphatically declared, and though every one laughed at him, every one liked him; and that is more than can be said of many saints and sages. He adored Polly, was dutifully kind to ma, and had stood T. Snow, Jr., in many an hour of tribulation, with fraternal fidelity. Though he had long blushed, sighed, and cast sheep's eyes at the idol of his affections, only till lately had he dared to bleat forth his passion. Polly loved him because she couldn't help it; but she was proud and wouldn't marry till Aunt Kipp's money was hers, or at least a sure prospect of it; and now even the prospect of a prospect was destroyed by that irrepressible Toady. They were talking of this, as the old lady suspected, and of course the following conversation afforded her intense satisfaction.

"It's a shame to torment us as she does, knowing how poor we are and how happy a little of her money would make us. I'm tired of being a slave to a cantankerous old woman just because she's rich. If it wan't for ma, I declare I'd wash my hands of her entirely and do the best I could for myself."

"Hooray for Polly! I always said let her old money go and be jolly without it," cried Toady, who, in his character of wounded hero, reposed with a lordly air on the sofa enjoying the fragrance of the opodeldoc with which his strained wrists were bandaged.

"It's on your account, children, that I bear with aunt's temper as I do. I don't want anything for myself, but I really think she owes it to your dear pa, who was devoted to her while he lived, to provide for his children when he couldn't;" after which remarkably spirited speech for her, Mrs. Snow dropped a tear and stitched away on a small trouser-leg which was suffering from a complicated compound fracture.

"Don't you worry about me, ma; I'll take care of myself and you too," remarked Toady, with the cheery belief in impossibilities which makes youth so charming.

"Now, Van, tell us what to do, for things have come to such a pass that we must either break away altogether or be galley-slaves as long as Aunt Kipp lives," said Polly, who was a good deal excited about the matter.

"Well, really, my dear, I don't know," hesitated Van, who did know what *he* wanted, but thought it might be selfish to urge it. "Have you tried to soften your aunt's heart?" he asked, after a moment's meditation.

"Good gracious, Van, she hasn't got any," cried Polly, who firmly believed it.

"It's hossified," thoughtfully remarked Toady, quite unconscious of any approach to a joke till every one giggled.

"You've had hossification enough for one

while, my lad," laughed Van. "Well, Polly, if the old lady has no heart you'd better let her go, for people without 'em aint worth much."

"That's a beautiful remark, Van, and a wise one. I just wish she could hear you make it, for she called you a fool," said Polly, irefully.

"Did she? Well, I don't mind, I'm used to it," returned Van, placidly; and so he was, for Polly called him a goose every day of her life, and he enjoyed it immensely.

"Then you think, dear, if we stopped worrying about aunt and her money, and worked instead of waited, that we shouldn't be any poorer and might be a great deal happier than we are now?" asked Polly, making a pretty little tableau as she put her hand through Van's arm and looked up at him with as much love, respect, and reliance as if he had been a manly six-footer with the face of an Apollo and the manners of a Chesterfield.

"Yes, my dear, I do, for it has troubled me a good deal to see you so badgered by that old — would you mind if I said, plague? Independence is a very nice thing, and poverty isn't half as bad as this sort of slavery. But you aint going to be poor, nor grub, nor worry about anything. We'll just be married, and take ma and Toady home, and be as jolly as grigs, and never bother about Mrs. K. again, — unless she loses her fortune, or gets sick, or comes to grief in any way. We'd lend her a hand then, wouldn't we, Polly?" and Van's mild face was pleasant to behold as he made the kindly proposition.

"Well, we'll think of it," said Polly, trying not to relent, but feeling that she was going very fast.

"Let's do it!" cried Toady, fired with the thought of privy conspiracy and rebellion. "Ma would be no end comfortable with Polly, and I'd help Van in the store, when I learned that confounded multiplication table," he added, with a groan; "and if Aunt Kipp comes a-visiting, we'll just sing out 'Not at home,' and let her bundle off again."

"It sounds very nice; but aunt will be dreadfully offended, and I don't wish to be ungrateful," said ma, brightening visibly.

"There's no ingratitude about it," cried Van. "She might have done everything to make you love and respect and admire her, and been a happy, useful, motherly, old soul; but she didn't choose to, and now she must take the consequences. No one cares for her, because she cares for nobody; her money's the plague of her life, and not a single heart will ache when she dies."

"Poor Aunt Kipp!" said Polly, softly.

Mrs. Snow echoed the words, and for a moment all thought pitifully of the woman whose life had given so little happiness, whose age had won so little reverence, and whose death would make so little regret. Even Toady had a kind thought for her, as he broke the silence, saying soberly : —

"You'd better put tails on my jackets, ma; then, the next time we get run away with, Aunt Kipp will have something to hold on by."

It was impossible to help laughing at the recollection of the old lady clutching at the boy till he had hardly a button left, and at the paternal air with which he now proposed a much-desired change of costume, as if intent on Aunt Kipp's future accommodation.

Under cover of the laugh, the old lady stole back to bed, wide awake, and with subjects enough to meditate upon now. The shaking-up had certainly done her good, for somehow the few virtues she possessed came to the surface, and the mental shower-bath just received had produced a salutary change. Polly wouldn't have doubted her aunt's possession of a heart, if she could have known the pain and loneliness that made it ache, as the old woman crept away; and Toady wouldn't have laughed if he had seen the tears on the face, between the big frills, as Aunt Kipp laid it on the pillow, muttering, drearily: —

"I might have been a happy, useful woman; but I didn't choose to, and now it's too late."

It *was* too late to be all she might have been, for the work of seventy selfish years couldn't be undone in a minute. But with regret, rose the sincere wish to earn a little love before the end came, and the old perversity gave a relish to the reformation, for even while she resolved to do the just and generous thing, she said to herself: —

"They say I've got no heart; I'll show 'em that I have: they don't want my money; I'll *make* 'em take it: they turn their backs on me; I'll just render myself so useful and agreeable that they can't do without me."

III.

Aunt Kipp sat bolt upright in the parlor, hemming a small handkerchief, adorned with a red ship, surrounded by an appropriate border of green monkeys. Toady suspected that this elegant article of dress was intended for him, and yearned to possess it; so, taking advantage of his mother's and Polly's absence, he strolled into the room, and, seating himself on a high, hard chair, folded his hands, crossed his legs, and asked for a story with the thirsting-for-knowledge air which little boys wear in the moral story-books.

Now Aunt Kipp had one soft place in her heart, though it *was* partially ossified, as she very truly declared, and Toady was enshrined therein. She thought there never was such a child, and loved him as she had done his father before him, though the rack wouldn't have forced her to confess it. She scolded, snubbed, and predicted he'd come to a bad end in public; but she forgave his naughtiest pranks, always brought him something when she came, and privately intended to make his future comfortable with half of her fortune. There was a dash and daring, a generosity and integrity, about the little fellow, that charmed her. Sophy was weak and low-spirited, Polly pretty and headstrong, and Aunt Kipp didn't think much of either of them; but Toady defied, distracted, and delighted her, and to Toady she clung, as the one sunshiny thing in her sour, selfish old age.

When he made his demure request, she looked at him, and her eyes began to twinkle, for the child's purpose was plainly seen in the loving glances cast upon the pictorial pocket-handkerchief.

"A story? Yes, I'll tell you one about a little boy who had a kind old — ahem! — grandma. She was rich, and hadn't made up her mind who she'd leave her money to. She was fond of the boy, — a deal fonder than he deserved, — for he was as mischievous a monkey as any that ever lived in a tree, with a curly tail. He put pepper in her snuff-box," — here Toady turned scarlet; "he cut up her best frisette to make a mane for his rocking-horse," — Toady opened his mouth impulsively, but shut it again without betraying himself; "he repeated rude things to her, and called her ' an old aggrewater,' " — here Toady wriggled in his chair, and gave a little gasp.

"If you are tired I won't go on," observed Aunt Kipp, mildly.

"I aint tired, 'm; it's a very interesting

story," replied Toady, with a gravity that nearly upset the old lady.

"Well, in spite of all this, that kind, good, forgiving grandma left that bad boy twenty thousand dollars when she died. What do you think of that?" asked Aunt Kipp, pausing suddenly with her sharp eye on him.

"I — I think she was a regular brick," cried Toady, holding on to the chair with both hands, as if that climax rather took him off his legs.

"And what did the boy do about it?" continued Aunt Kipp, curiously.

"He bought a velocipede, and gave his sister half, and paid his ma's rent, and put a splendid marble cherakin over the old lady, and had a jolly good time, and —"

"What in the world is a cherakin?" laughed Aunt Kipp, as Toady paused for breath.

"Why, don't you know? It's a angel cryin', or pointin' up, or flappin' his wings. They have 'em over dead folks' graves; and I'll give you the biggest one I can find when you die. But I aint in a *very* great hurry to have you."

"Thankee, dear; I'm in no hurry myself. But, Toady, the boy did wrong in giving his sister half; she didn't deserve *any;* and the grandma left word she wasn't to have a penny of it."

"Really?" cried the boy, with a troubled face.

"Yes, really. If he gave her any he lost it all; the old lady said so. Now what do you think?" asked Aunt Kipp, who found it impossible to pardon Polly, — perhaps because she was young, and pretty, and much beloved.

Toady's eyes kindled, and his red cheeks grew redder still, as he cried out defiantly: —

"I think she was a selfish pig, — don't you?"

"No, I don't, sir; and I'm sure that little boy

wasn't such a fool as to lose the money. He minded his grandma's wishes, and kept it all."

"No, he didn't," roared Toady, tumbling off his chair in great excitement. "He just chucked it out a winder, and smashed the old cherakin all to bits."

Aunt Kipp dropped her work with a shrill squeak, for she thought the boy was dangerous, as he stood before her sparring away at nothing as the only vent for his indignation.

"It aint an interesting story," he bawled; "and I won't hear any more; and I won't have your money if I mayn't go halves with Polly; and I'll work to earn more'n that, and we'll all be jolly together, and you may give your twenty thousand to the old rag-bags, and so I tell you, Aunt Kipp."

"Why, Toady, my boy, what's the matter?"

cried a mild voice at the door, as young Lamb came trotting up to the rescue.

"Never you mind, Baa-baa; I shan't do it; and it's a mean shame Polly can't have half; then she could marry you and be no end happy," blubbered Toady, running to try to hide his tears of disappointment in the coat-skirts of his friend.

"Mr. Lamb, I suppose you *are* that misguided young man?" said Aunt Kipp, as if it was a personal insult to herself.

"Van Bahr Lamb, ma'am, if you please. Yes, thank you," murmured Baa-baa, bowing, blushing, and rumpling his curly fleece in bashful trepidation.

"Don't thank me," cried the old lady. "I'm not going to give you anything, — far from it. I object to you altogether. What business have you to come courting my niece?"

"Because I love her, ma'am," returned Van, with unexpected spirit.

"No, you don't; you want her money, or rather my money. She depends on it; but you'll both be disappointed, for she won't have a penny of it," cried Aunt Kipp, who, in spite of her good resolutions, found it impossible to be amiable all at once.

"I'm glad of it!" burst out Van, indignant at her accusation. "I didn't want Polly for the money; I always doubted if she got it; and I never wished her to make herself a slave to anybody. I've got enough for all, if we're careful; and when my share of the Van Bahr property comes, we shall live in clover."

"What's that? What property are you talking of?" demanded Aunt Kipp, pricking up her ears.

"The great Van Bahr estate, ma'am. There has been a long lawsuit about it, but it's nearly settled, and there isn't much doubt that we shall get it. I am the last of our branch, and my share will be a big one."

"Oh, indeed! I wish you joy," said Aunt Kipp, with sudden affability; for she adored wealth, like a few other persons in the world. "But suppose you don't get it, how then?"

"Then I shall try to be contented with my salary of two thousand, and make Polly as happy as I can. Money don't *always* make people happy or agreeable, I find." And Van looked at Aunt Kipp in a way that would have made her hair stand erect if she'd had any. She stared at him a moment, then, obeying one of the odd whims that made an irascible weathercock of her, she said, abruptly: —

"If you had capital should you go into business for yourself, Mr. Lambkin?"

"Yes, ma'am, at once," replied Van, promptly.

"Suppose you lost the Van Bahr money, and some one offered you a tidy little sum to start with, would you take it?'

"It would depend upon who made the offer, ma'am," said Van, looking more like a sheep than ever, as he stood poking his head forward, and staring in blank surprise.

"Suppose it was me, wouldn't you take it?" asked Aunt Kipp, blandly, for the new fancy pleased her.

"No, thank you, ma'am," said Van, decidedly.

"And why not, pray?" cried the old lady, with a shrillness that made him jump, and Toady back to the door precipitately.

"Because, if you'll excuse my speaking plainly, I think you owe anything you may have to spare to your niece, Mrs. Snow;" and, having freed his mind, Van joined Toady, ready to fly if necessary.

"You're an idiot, sir," began Aunt Kipp, in a rage again.

"Thank you, ma'am." And Van actually laughed and bowed in return for the compliment.

"Hold your tongue, sir," snapped the old lady. "You're a fool and Sophy is another. She's no strength of mind, no sense about anything; and would make ducks and drakes of my money in less than no time if I gave it to her, as I've thought of doing."

"Mrs. Kipp, you forget who you are speaking to. Mrs. Snow's sons love and respect her if you don't, and they won't hear anything untrue or unkind said of a good woman, a devoted mother, and an almost friendless widow."

Van wasn't a dignified man at all, but as he said that with a sudden flash of his mild eyes, there was something in his face and manner that daunted Aunt Kipp more than the small fist belligerently shaken at her from behind the sofa. The poor old soul was cross, and worried, and ashamed of herself, and being as feeble-minded as Sophy in many respects, she suddenly burst into tears, and, covering her face with the gay handkerchief, cried as if bent on floating the red ship in a sea of salt water without delay.

"I'm a poor, lonely, abused old woman," she moaned, with a green monkey at each eye. "No one loves me, or minds me, or thanks me when I want to help 'em. My money's only a worriment and a burden, and I don't know what to do with it, for them I don't want to leave it to ought to have it, and them I do like won't take it. Oh, deary me, what *shall* I do! what shall I do!"

"Shall I tell you, ma'am?" asked Van, gently, for, though she was a very provoking old party, he pitied and wished to help her.

A nod and a gurgle seemed to give consent,

and, boldly advancing, Van said, with a blush and a stammer, and a somewhat mild expression, but a very hearty voice: —

"I think, ma'am, if you'd do the right thing with your money you'd be at ease and find it saved a deal of worry all round. Give it to Mrs. Snow; she deserves it, poor lady, for she's had a hard time, and done her duty faithfully. Don't wait till you are — that is till you — well, till you in point of fact die, ma'am. Give it now, and enjoy the happiness it will make. Give it kindly, let 'em see you're glad to do it, and I am sure you'll find 'em grateful; I'm sure you won't be lonely any more, or feel that you aint loved and thanked. Try it, ma'am, just try it," cried Van, getting excited by the picture he drew. "And I give you my word I'll do my best to respect and love you like a son, ma'am."

He knew that he was promising a great deal,

but for Polly's sake he felt that he could make even that Herculean effort. Aunt Kipp was surprised and touched; but the contrary old lady couldn't make up her mind to yield so soon, and wouldn't have done it if Toady hadn't taken her by storm. Having a truly masculine horror of tears, and a very tender heart under his tailless jacket, and being much "tumbled up and down in his own mind" by the events of the week, the poor little lad felt nerved to attempt any novel enterprise, even that of voluntarily embracing Aunt Kipp. First a grimy little hand came on her shoulder, as she sat sniffing behind the handkerchief; then, peeping out, she saw an apple-cheeked face very near her own, with eyes full of pity, penitence, and affection; and then she heard a choky little voice say earnestly: —

"Don't cry, aunty; I'm sorry I was rude. Please be good to ma and Polly, and I'll love and take care of you, and stand by you like a trump. Yes, I'll — I'll *kiss* you, I will, by George!" And with one promiscuous plunge the Spartan boy cast himself into her arms.

That finished Aunt Kipp; she hugged him close, and cried out, with a salute that went off like a pistol-shot: —

"Oh, my dear, my dear! this is better than a dozen cherakins!"

When Toady emerged, somewhat flushed and tumbled, ma, Polly, and Van, were looking on with faces full of wonder, doubt, and satisfaction. To be an object of interest was agreeable to Aunt Kipp; and, as her old heart was really softened, she met them with a gracious smile, and extended the olive-branch generally.

"Sophy, I shall give my money to *you* at once and entirely, only asking that you'll let me stay with you when Polly's gone. I'll do my best to be agreeable, and you'll bear with me, because I'm a cranky, solitary old woman, and I loved your husband."

Mrs. Snow hugged her on the spot, and gushed, of course, murmuring thanks, welcomes, and promises in one grateful burst.

"Polly, I forgive you; I consent to your marriage, and will provide your wedding finery. Mr. Lamb you are not a fool, but a very excellent young man. I thank you for saving my life, and I wish you well with all my heart. You needn't say anything. I'm far from strong, and all this agitation is shortening my life."

Polly and Van shook her hand heartily, and beamed upon each other like a pair of infatuated turtle-doves with good prospects.

"Theodore, you are as near an angel as a boy can be. Put a name to whatever you most wish for in the world, and it's yours," said Aunt Kipp, dramatically waving the rest away.

With his short legs wide apart, his hands behind him, and his rosy face as round and radiant as a rising sun, Toady stood before the fire surveying the scene with the air of a man who has successfully carried through a difficult and dangerous undertaking, and wasn't proud. His face brightened, then fell, as he heaved a sigh, and answered, with a shake of his curly head: —

"You can't give me what I want most. There's three things, and I've got to wait for 'em all."

"Gracious me, what are they?" cried the old lady, good-naturedly, for she felt better already.

"A mustache, a beaver, *and* a sweetheart," answered Toady, with his eyes fixed wistfully on Baa-baa, who possessed all these blessings, and was particularly enjoying the latter at that moment.

How Aunt Kipp did laugh at this early budding of romance in her pet! And all the rest joined her, for Toady's sentimental air was irresistible.

"You precocious chick! I dare say you will have 'em all before we know where we are. Never mind, deary; you shall have my little watch, and the silver teapot with the *boar's* head on the lid," answered the old lady, in high good-humor. "You needn't blush, Polly; I don't bear malice; so let's forget and forgive. I shall settle things to-morrow, and have a free mind. You are welcome to my money, and I hope I shall live to see you all enjoy it."

So she did; for she lived to see Sophy plump, cheery, and care-free; Polly surrounded by a flock of Lambkins; Van in possession of a generous slice of the Van Bahr fortune; Toady revelling in the objects of his desire; and, best of all, she lived to find that it is never too late to make one's self useful, happy and beloved.

PSYCHE'S ART.

"Handsome is that handsome does."

I.

Once upon a time there raged in a certain city one of those fashionable epidemics which occasionally attack our youthful population. It wasn't the music mania, nor gymnastic convulsions, nor that wide-spread malady, croquet. Neither was it one of the new dances which, like a tarantula-bite, set every one a-twirling, nor stage madness, nor yet that American lecturing influenza which yearly sweeps over the land. No, it was a new disease called the Art

fever, and it attacked the young women of the community with great violence.

Nothing but time could cure it, and it ran its course to the dismay, amusement, or edification of the beholders, for its victims did all manner of queer things in their delirium. They besieged potteries for clay, drove Italian plaster-workers out of their wits with unexecutable orders, got neuralgia and rheumatism sketching perched on fences and trees like artistic hens, and caused a rise in the price of bread, paper, and charcoal, by their order in crayoning. They covered canvas with the expedition of scene-painters, had classes, lectures, receptions, and exhibitions, made models of each other, and rendered their walls hideous with bad likenesses of all their friends. Their conversation ceased to be intelligible to the uninitiated, and they prattled prettily of "chiaro-oscuro, French sauce, refraction of the angle of the eye, seventh spinus process, depth and juiciness of color, tender touch, and a good tone." Even in dress the artistic disorder was visible; some cast aside crinoline altogether, and stalked about with a severe simplicity of outline worthy of Flaxman. Others flushed themselves with scarlet, that no landscape which they adorned should be without some touch of Turner's favorite tint. Some were *blue* in every sense of the word, and the heads of all were adorned with classic braids, curls tied Hebe-wise, or hair dressed à la hurricane.

It was found impossible to keep them safe at home, and, as the fever grew, these harmless maniacs invaded the sacred retreats where artists of the other sex did congregate, startling those anchorites with visions of large-eyed damsels bearing portfolios in hands delicately begrimed with crayon, chalk, and clay, gliding through the corridors hitherto haunted only by shabby paletots, shadowy hats, and cigar smoke. This irruption was borne with manly fortitude, not to say cheerfulness, for studio doors stood hospitably open as the fair invaders passed, and studies from life were generously offered them in glimpses of picturesque gentlemen posed before easels, brooding over master-pieces in "a divine despair," or attitudinizing upon couches as if exhausted by the soarings of genius.

An atmosphere of romance began to pervade the old buildings when the girls came, and nature and art took turns. There were peepings and whisperings, much stifled laughter and whisking in and out; not to mention the accidental rencontres, small services, and eye telegrams, which somewhat lightened the severe studies of all parties.

Half-a-dozen young victims of this malady met daily in one of the cells of a great art beehive called "Raphel's Rooms," and devoted their shining hours to modelling fancy heads, gossiping the while; for the poor things found the road to fame rather dull and dusty without such verbal sprinklings.

"Psyche Dean, you've had an adventure! I see it in your face; so tell it at once, for we are as stupid as owls here to-day," cried one of the sisterhood, as a bright-eyed girl entered with some precipitation.

"I dropped my portfolio, and a man picked it up, that's all," replied Psyche, hurrying on her gray linen pinafore.

"That won't do; I know something interesting happened, for you've been blushing, and you look brisker than usual this morning," said the first speaker, polishing off the massive nose of her Homer.

"It wasn't anything," began Psyche, a little reluctantly. "I was coming up in a hurry when I ran against a man coming down in a hurry.

My portfolio slipped, and my papers went flying all about the landing. Of course we both laughed and begged pardon, and I began to pick them up, but he wouldn't let me; so I held the book while he collected the sketches. I saw him glance at them as he did so, and that made me blush, for they are wretched things, you know."

"Not a bit of it; they are capital, and you are a regular genius, as we all agree," cut in the Homeric Miss Cutter.

"Never tell people they are geniuses unless you wish to spoil them," returned Psyche, severely. "Well, when the portfolio was put to rights I was going on, but he fell to picking up a little bunch of violets I had dropped; you know I always wear a posy into town to give me inspiration. I didn't care for the dusty flowers, and told him so, and scrambled away before any one came. At the top of the stairs I peeped over the railing, and there he was, gathering up every one of those half-dead violets as carefully as if they had been tea-roses."

"Psyche Dean, you have met your fate this day!" exclaimed a third damsel, with straw-colored tresses, and a good deal of weedy shrubbery in her hat, which gave an Ophelia-like expression to her sentimental countenance.

Psyche frowned and shook her head as if half sorry she had told her little story.

"Was he handsome?" asked Miss Larkins, the believer in fate.

"I didn't particularly observe."

"It was the red-headed man, whom we call Titian; he's always on the stairs."

"No, it wasn't; his hair was brown and curly," cried Psyche, innocently falling into the trap.

"Like Peerybingle's baby when its cap was

taken off," quoted Miss Dickenson, who pined to drop the last two letters of her name.

"Was it Murillo, the black-eyed one?" asked the fair Cutter, for the girls had a name for all the attitudinizers and promenaders whom they oftenest met.

"No, he had gray eyes, and very fine ones they were too," answered Psyche, adding, as if to herself, "he looked as I imagine Michael Angelo might have looked when young."

"Had he a broken nose like the great Mike?" asked an irreverent damsel.

"If he had, no one would mind it, for his head is splendid; he took his hat off, so I had a fine view. He isn't handsome, but he'll *do* something," said Psyche, prophetically, as she recalled the strong, ambitious face which she had often observed, but never mentioned before.

"Well, dear, considering that you didn't

'particularly look' at the man, you've given us a very good idea of his appearance. We'll call him Michael Angelo, and he shall be your idol. I prefer stout old Rembrandt myself, and Larkie adores that dandefied Raphael," said the lively Cutter, slapping away at Homer's bald pate energetically, as she spoke.

"Raphael is a dear, but Rubens is more to my taste now," returned Miss Larkins. "He was in the hall yesterday talking with Sir Joshua, who had his inevitable umbrella, like a true Englishman. Just as I came up, the umbrella fell right before me. I started back; Sir Joshua laughed, but Rubens said, 'Deuce take it!' and caught up the umbrella, giving me a never-to-be-forgotten look. It was perfectly thrilling."

"Which, — the umbrella, the speech, or the look?" asked Psyche, who was not sentimental.

"Ah, you have no soul for art in nature, and

nature in art," sighed the amber-tressed Larkins. "I have, for I feed upon a glance, a tint, a curve, with exquisite delight. Rubens is adorable (*as a study*); that lustrous eye, that night of hair, that sumptuous cheek, are perfect. He only needs a cloak, lace collar, and slouching hat to be the genuine thing."

"This isn't the genuine thing by any means. What *does* it need?" said Psyche, looking with a despondent air at the head on her stand.

Many would have pronounced it a clever thing; the nose was strictly Greek, the chin curved upward gracefully, the mouth was sweetly haughty, the brow classically smooth and low, and the breezy hair well done. But something was wanting; Psyche felt that, and could have taken her Venus by the dimpled shoulders, and given her a hearty shake, if that would have put strength and spirit into the lifeless face.

"Now *I* am perfectly satisfied with my

Apollo, though you all insist that it is the image of Theodore Smythe. He says so himself, and assures me it will make a sensation when we exhibit," remarked Miss Larkins, complacently caressing the ambrosial locks of her Smythified Phebus.

"What shall you do if it don't?" asked Miss Cutter, with elegance.

"I shall feel that I have mistaken my sphere, shall drop my tools, veil my bust, and cast myself into the arms of Nature, since Art rejects me," replied Miss Larkins, with a tragic gesture and an expression which strongly suggested that in her eyes Nature meant Theodore.

"She must have capacious arms if she is to receive all Art's rejected admirers. Shall I be one of them?"

Psyche put the question to herself as she turned to work, but somehow ambitious aspirations were not in a flourishing condition that morning; her heart was not in tune, and head and hands sympathized. Nothing went well, for certain neglected home-duties had dogged her into town, and now worried her more than dust, or heat, or the ceaseless clatter of tongues. Tom, Dick, and Harry's unmended hose persisted in dancing a spectral jig before her mental eye, mother's querulous complaints spoilt the song she hummed to cheer herself, and little May's wistful face put the goddess of beauty entirely out of countenance.

"It s no use; I can't work till the clay is wet again. Where is Giovanni?" she asked, throwing down her tools with a petulant gesture and a dejected air.

"He is probably playing truant in the empty upper rooms as usual. I can't wait for him any longer, so I'm doing his work myself," answered Miss Dickenson, who was tenderly winding a wet bandage round her Juno's face, one side of which was so much plumper than the other that it looked as if the Queen of Olympus was being hydropathically treated for a severe fit of ague.

"I'll go and find the little scamp; a run will do me good; so will a breath of air and a view of the park from the upper windows."

Doffing her apron, Psyche strolled away up an unfrequented staircase to the empty apartments, which seemed to be too high even for the lovers of High Art. On the western side they were shady and cool, and, leaning from one of the windows, Psyche watched the feathery tree-tops ruffled by the balmy wind, that brought spring odors from the hills, lying green and sunny far away. Silence and solitude were such pleasant companions that the girl forgot herself, till a shrill whistle disturbed her day-dreams, and reminded her what she came for. Following the sound she found the little Italian errand-boy busily uncovering a clay model which stood in the middle of a scantily furnished room near by.

"He is not here; come and look; it is greatly beautiful," cried Giovanni, beckoning with an air of importance.

Psyche did look and speedily forgot both her errand and herself. It was the figure of a man, standing erect, and looking straight before him with a wonderfully life-like expression. It was neither a mythological nor a historical character, Psyche thought, and was glad of it, being tired to death of gods and heroes. She soon ceased to wonder what it was, feeling only the indescribable charm of something higher than beauty. Small as her knowledge was, she could see and enjoy the power visible in every part of it; the accurate anatomy of the vigorous limbs, the grace of the pose, the strength and spirit in the countenance, clay though it was. A majestic figure, but the spell lay in the face, which, while it suggested the divine, was full of human truth and tenderness, for pain and passion seemed to have passed over it and a humility half-pathetic, a courage half-heroic, seemed to have been born from some great loss or woe.

How long she stood there Psyche did not know. Giovanni went away unseen, to fill his water-pail, and in the silence she just stood and looked. Her eyes kindled, her color rose, despondency and discontent vanished, and her soul was in her face, for she loved beauty passionately, and all that was best and truest in her did honor to the genius of the unknown worker.

"If I could do a thing like that I'd die happy!" she exclaimed, impetuously, as a feeling of despair came over her at the thought of her own poor attempts.

"Who did it, Giovanni?" she asked, still looking up at the grand face with unsatisfied eyes.

"Paul Gage."

It was not the boy's voice, and, with a start, Psyche turned to see her Michael Angelo, standing in the door-way attentively observing her. Being too full of artless admiration to think of herself just yet, she neither blushed nor apologized, but looked straight at him, saying heartily: —

"You have done a wonderful piece of work, and I envy you more than I can tell."

The enthusiasm in her face, the frankness of her manner, seemed to please him, for there was no affectation about either. He gave her a keen, kind glance out of the "fine gray eyes," a little bow, and a grateful smile, saying quietly: —

"Then my Adam is not a failure in spite of his fall?"

Psyche turned from the sculptor to his model with increased admiration in her face, and earnestness in her voice, as she exclaimed, delighted : —

"Adam! I might have known it was he. O sir, you have indeed succeeded, for you have given that figure the power and pathos of the first man who sinned and suffered, and began again."

"Then I am satisfied." That was all he said, but the look he gave his work was a very eloquent one, for it betrayed that he had paid the price of success in patience and privation, labor and hope.

"What can one do to learn your secret?" asked the girl wistfully, for there was nothing in the man's manner to disturb her self-forgetful mood, but much to foster it, because to the solitary worker this confiding guest was as welcome as the doves who often hopped in at his window.

"Work and wait, and meantime feed heart,

soul, and imagination with the best food one can get," he answered slowly, finding it impossible to give a receipt for genius.

"I can work and wait a long time to gain my end; but I don't know where to find the food you speak of," she answered, looking at him like a hungry child.

"I wish I could tell you, but each needs different fare, and each must look for it in different places."

The kindly tone and the sympathizing look, as well as the lines in his forehead, and a few gray hairs among the brown, gave Psyche courage to say more.

"I love beauty so much that I not only want to possess it myself, but to gain the power of seeing it in all things, and the art of reproducing it with truth. I have tried very hard to do it, but something is wanting; and in spite of my intense desire I never get on."

As she spoke the girl's eyes filled and fell in spite of herself, and turning a little with sudden shamefacedness she saw, lying on the table beside her among other scraps in manuscript and print, the well-known lines: —

> "I slept, and dreamed that life was beauty;
> I woke, and found that life was duty.
> Was thy dream then a shadowy lie?
> Toil on, sad heart, courageously,
> And thou shalt find thy dream to be
> A noonday light and truth to thee."

She knew them at a glance, had read them many times, but now they came home to her with sudden force, and, seeing that his eye had followed hers, she said in her impulsive fashion: —

"Is doing one's duty a good way to feed heart, soul, and imagination?"

As if he had caught a glimpse of what was

going on in her mind, Paul answered emphatically : -

"Excellent; for if one is good, one is happy, and if happy, one can work well. Moulding character is the highest sort of sculpture, and all of us should learn that art before we touch clay or marble."

He spoke with the energy of a man who believed what he said, and did his best to be worthy of the rich gift bestowed upon him. The sight of her violets in a glass of water, and Giovanni staring at her with round eyes, suddenly recalled Psyche to a sense of the proprieties which she had been innocently outraging for the last ten minutes. A sort of panic seized her; she blushed deeply, retreated precipitately to the door, and vanished murmuring thanks and apologies as she went.

"Did you find him? I thought you had forgotten," said Miss Dickenson, now hard at work.

"Yes, I found him. No, I shall not forget," returned Psyche, thinking of Gage, not Giovanni.

She stood before her work eying it intently for several minutes; then, with an expression of great contempt for the whole thing, she suddenly tilted her cherished Venus on to the floor, gave the classical face a finishing crunch, and put on her hat in a decisive manner, saying briefly to the dismayed damsels: —

"Good-by, girls; I shan't come any more, for I'm going to work at home hereafter."

II.

The prospect of pursuing artistic studies at home was not brilliant, as one may imagine when I mention that Psyche's father was a painfully prosaic man, wrapt in flannel, so to speak; for his woollen mills left him no time for anything but sleep, food, and newspapers. Mrs. Dean was one of those exasperating women who pervade their mansions like a domestic steam-engine one week and take to their sofas the next, absorbed by fidgets and foot-stoves, shawls and lamentations. There were three riotous and robust young brothers, whom it is unnecessary to describe except by stating that they were *boys* in the broadest sense of that delightful word. There was a feeble little sister, whose patient, suffering face demanded constant love and care to mitigate the weariness of a life of pain. And last, but not least by any means, there were two Irish ladies, who, with the best intentions imaginable, produced a universal state of topsy-turvyness when left to themselves for a moment.

But being very much in earnest about doing her duty, not because it *was* her duty, but as a means toward an end, Psyche fell to work with a will, hoping to serve both masters at once. So she might have done, perhaps, if flesh and blood had been as plastic as clay, but the live models were so exacting in their demands upon her time and strength, that the poor statues went to the wall. Sculpture and sewing, calls and crayons, Ruskin and receipt-books, didn't work well together, and poor Psyche found duties and desires desperately antagonistic. Take a day as a sample.

"The washing and ironing is well over, thank

goodness, ma used up and quiet, the boys out of the way, and May comfortable, so I'll indulge myself in a blissful day after my own heart," Psyche said, as she shut herself into her little studio, and prepared to enjoy a few hours of hard study and happy day-dreams.

With a book on her lap, and her own round, white arm going through all manner of queer evolutions, she was placidly repeating, "Deltoids, Biceps, Triceps, Pronator, Supinator, Palmanis, Flexor carpi ulnaris —"

"Here's Flexis what-you-call-ums for you," interrupted a voice, which began in a shrill falsetto and ended in a gruff bass, as a flushed, dusty, long-legged boy burst in, with a bleeding hand obligingly extended for inspection.

"Mercy on us, Harry. what have you done to yourself now? Split your fingers with a cricket-ball again?" cried Psyche, as her arms went up and her book went down.

"No, sir. I just pitched into one of the fellows because he got mad and said pa was going to fail."

"O Harry, is he?"

"Course he isn't! It's hard times for every one, but pa will pull through like a brick. No use to try and explain it all; girls can't understand business; so you just tie me up, and don't bother," was the characteristic reply of the young man, who, being three years her junior, of course treated the weaker vessel with lordly condescension.

"What a dreadful wound! I hope nothing is broken, for I haven't studied the hand much yet, and may do mischief doing it up," said Psyche, examining the great grimy paw with tender solicitude.

"Much good your biceps, and deltoids, and things do you, if you can't right up a little cut like that," squeaked the ungrateful hero.

"I'm not going to be a surgeon, thank Heaven; I intend to make perfect hands and arms, not mend damaged ones," retorted Psyche, in a dignified tone, somewhat marred by a great piece of court-plaster on her tongue.

"I should say a surgeon could improve *that* perfect thing, if he didn't die a-laughing before he began," growled Harry, pointing with a scornful grin at a clay arm humpy with muscles all carefully developed in the wrong places.

"Don't hoot, Hal, for you don't know anything about it. Wait a few years and see if you're not proud of me."

"Sculp away then, do your prettiest, and I'll hurrah for your mud-pies like a good one;" with which cheering promise the youth departed, having effectually disturbed his sister's peaceful mood.

Anxious thoughts of her father rendered "biceps, deltoids, and things" uninteresting, and, hoping to compose her mind, she took up The Old Painters and went on with the story of Claude Lorraine. She had just reached the tender scene where : — .

"Calista gazed with enthusiasm, while she looked like a being of heaven rather than earth. 'My friend,' she cried, 'I read in thy picture thy immortality!' As she spoke, her head sunk upon his bosom, and it was several moments before Claude perceived that he supported a lifeless form."

"How sweet!" said Psyche, with a romantic sigh.

"Faith, and swate it is thin!" echoed Katy, whose red head had just appeared round the half-opened door. "It's gingybread I'm making the day, miss, and will I be puttin' purlash or sallyrathis into it, if ye plase?"

"Purlash by all means," returned the girl, keeping her countenance, fearing to enrage Katy by a laugh; for the angry passions of the redhaired one rose more quickly than her bread. As she departed with alacrity to add a spoonful of starch and a pinch of whiting to her cake, Psyche, feeling better for her story and her smile, put on her bib and paper cap and fell to work on the deformed arm. An hour of bliss, then came a ring at the door-bell, followed by Biddy to announce callers, and add that as "the mistress was in her bed, miss must go and take care of 'em." Whereat "miss" cast down her tools in despair, threw her cap one way, her bib another, and went in to her guests with anything but a rapturous welcome.

Dinner being accomplished after much rushing up and down stairs with trays and messages for Mrs. Dean, Psyche fled again to her studio, ordering no one to approach under pain of a scolding. All went well till, going in search of something, she found her little sister sitting on the floor with her cheek against the studio door.

"I didn't mean to be naughty, Sy, but ma's asleep, and the boys all gone, so I just came to be near you; it's so lonely everywhere," she said, apologetically, as she lifted up the heavy head that always ached.

"The boys are very thoughtless. Come in and stay with me; you are such a mouse you won't disturb me. Wouldn't you like to play be a model, and let me draw your arm, and tell you all about the nice little bones and muscles?" asked Psyche, who had the fever very strong upon her just then.

May didn't look as if the proposed amusement overwhelmed her with delight, but meekly consented to be perched upon a high stool with one arm propped up by a dropsical plaster cherub, while Psyche drew busily, feeling that duty and pleasure were being delightfully combined.

"Can't you hold your arm still, child? It shakes so I can't get it right," she said, rather impatiently.

"No, it will tremble, 'cause it's weak. I try hard, Sy, but there don't seem to be any strongness in me lately."

"That's better; keep it so a few minutes and I'll be done," cried the artist, forgetting that a few minutes may seem ages.

"My arm is so thin you can see the bunches nicely, — can't you?"

"Yes, dear."

Psyche glanced up at the wasted limb and when she drew again there was a blur before her eyes for a minute.

"I wish I was as fat as this white boy; but I get thinner every day somehow, and pretty soon there won't be any of me left but my little bones," said the child, looking at the winged cherub with sorrowful envy.

"Don't, my darling; don't say that," cried Psyche, dropping her work with a sudden pang at her heart. "I'm a sinful, selfish girl to keep you here; you're weak for want of air; come out and see the chickens, and pick dandelions, and have a good romp with the boys."

The weak arms were strong enough to clasp Psyche's neck, and the tired face brightened beautifully as the child exclaimed, with grateful delight:—

"Oh, I'd like it very much! I wanted to go dreadfully; but everybody is so busy all the time. I don't want to play, Sy; but just to lie on the grass with my head in your lap while you tell stories and draw me pretty things as you used to."

The studio was deserted all that afternoon, for Psyche sat in the orchard drawing squirrels on the wall, pert robbins hopping by, buttercups and mosses, elves and angels; while May lay contentedly enjoying sun and air, sisterly care, and the "pretty things" she loved so well. Psyche did not find the task a hard one; for this time her heart was in it, and if she needed any reward she surely found it; for the little face on her knee lost its weary look, and the peace and beauty of nature soothed her own troubled spirit, cheered her heart, and did her more good than hours of solitary study.

Finding, much to her own surprise, that her fancy was teeming with lovely conceits, she did hope for a quiet evening. But ma wanted a dish of gossip, pa must have his papers read to him, the boys had lessons and rips and grievances to be attended to, May's lullaby could not be forgotten, and the maids had to be looked after, lest burly "cousins" should be hidden in the boiler, or lucifer matches among the shavings. So Psyche's day ended, leaving her very tired, rather discouraged, and almost heart-sick with the shadow of a coming sorrow.

All summer she did her best, but accomplished very little as she thought; yet this was the teaching she most needed, and in time she came to see it. In the autumn May died, whispering with her arms about her sister's neck: —

"You make me so happy, Sy, I wouldn't mind the pain if I could stay a little longer. But if I can't, good-by, dear, good-by."

Her last look and word and kiss were all for Psyche, who felt then with grateful tears that her summer had not been wasted; for the smile upon the little dead face was more to her than any marble perfection her hands could have carved.

In the solemn pause which death makes in every family, Psyche said, with the sweet self-forgetfulness of a strong yet tender nature: —

"I must not think of myself, but try to comfort them;" and with this resolution she gave herself heart and soul to duty, never thinking of reward.

A busy, anxious, humdrum winter, for, as Harry said, "it was hard times for every one." Mr. Dean grew gray with the weight of business cares about which he never spoke; Mrs. Dean, laboring under the delusion that an invalid was a necessary appendage to the family, installed herself in the place the child's death left vacant, and the boys needed much comforting, for the poor lads never knew how much they loved "the baby" till the little chair stood empty. All turned to Sy for help and consolation, and her strength seemed to increase with the demand upon it. Patience and cheerfulness, courage and skill, came at her call like good fairies who had bided their time. House-keeping ceased to be hateful, and peace reigned in parlor and kitchen, while Mrs. Dean, shrouded in shawls, read Hahnemann's Lesser Writings on her sofa. Mr. Dean sometimes forgot his mills when a bright face came to meet him, a gentle hand smoothed the wrinkles out of his anxious forehead, and a daughterly heart sympathized with all his cares. The boys found home very pleasant with Sy always there ready to "lend a hand," whether it was to make fancy ties, help conjugate "a confounded verb," pull candy, or sing sweetly in the twilight when all thought of little May and grew quiet.

The studio door remained locked till her brothers begged Psyche to open it and make a bust of the child. A flush of joy swept over her face at the request, and her patient eyes grew bright and eager, as a thirsty traveller's might at the sight or sound of water. Then it faded as she shook her head, saying, with a regretful sigh, "I'm afraid I've lost the little skill I ever had."

But she tried, and with great wonder and delight discovered that she could work as she had never done before. She thought the newly found power lay in her longing to see the little face again; for it grew like magic under her loving hands, while every tender memory, sweet thought, and devout hope she had ever cherished, seemed to lend their aid. But when it was done and welcomed with tears and smiles, and praise more precious than any the world could give, then Psyche said within herself like one who saw light at last: —

"He was right; doing one's duty *is* the way to feed heart, soul, and imagination; for if one is good, one is happy, and if happy, one can work well."

III.

"She broke her head, and went home to come no more," was Giovanni's somewhat startling answer when Paul asked about Psyche, finding that he no longer met her on the stairs or in the halls. He understood what the boy meant, and with an approving nod turned to his work again, saying, "I like that! If there is any power in her, she has taken the right way to find it out, I suspect."

How she prospered he never asked; for, though he met her more than once that year, the interviews were brief ones in street, concert-room, or picture-gallery, and she carefully avoided speaking of herself. But, possessing the gifted eyes which can look below the surface of things, he detected in the girl's face some-

thing better than beauty, though each time he saw it, it looked older and more thoughtful, often anxious and sad.

"She is getting on," he said to himself with a cordial satisfaction which gave his manner a friendliness as grateful to Psyche as his wise reticence.

Adam was finished at last, proved a genuine success, and Paul heartily enjoyed the well-earned reward for years of honest work. One blithe May morning, he slipped early into the art-gallery, where the statue now stood, to look at his creation with paternal pride. He was quite alone with the stately figure that shone white against the purple draperies and seemed to offer him a voiceless welcome from its marble lips. He gave it one loving look, and then forgot it, for at the feet of his Adam lay a handful of wild violets, with the dew still on them. A sudden smile broke over his face as he took them up, with the thought, "She has been here and found my work good."

For several moments he stood thoughtfully turning the flowers to and fro in his hands; then, as if deciding some question within himself, he said, still smiling:—

"It is just a year since she went home; she must have accomplished something in that time; I'll take the violets as a sign that I may go and ask her what."

He knew she lived just out of the city, between the river and the mills, and as he left the streets behind him, he found more violets blooming all along the way like flowery guides to lead him right. Greener grew the road, balmier blew the wind, and blither sang the birds, as he went on enjoying his holiday with the zest of a boy, until he reached a most attractive little path winding away across the fields. The gate swung invitingly open, and all the ground before it was blue with violets. Still following their guidance he took the narrow path, till, coming to a mossy stone beside a brook, he sat down to listen to the blackbirds singing deliciously in the willows overhead. Close by the stone, half hidden in the grass lay a little book, and, taking it up, he found it was a pocket-diary. No name appeared on the fly-leaf, and, turning the pages to find some clue to its owner, he read here and there enough to give him glimpses into an innocent and earnest heart which seemed to be learning some hard lesson patiently. Only near the end did he find the clue in words of his own, spoken long ago, and a name. Then, though longing intensely to know more, he shut the little book and went on, showing by his altered face that the simple record of a girl's life had touched him deeply.

Soon an old house appeared nestling to the

hillside with the river shining in the low green meadows just before it.

"She lives there," he said, with as much certainty as if the pansies by the door-stone spelt her name, and, knocking, he asked for Psyche.

"She's gone to town, but I expect her home every minute." "Ask the gentleman to walk in and wait, Katy," cried a voice from above, where the whisk of skirts was followed by the appearance of an inquiring eye over the banisters.

The gentleman did walk in, and while he waited looked about him. The room, though very simply furnished, had a good deal of beauty in it, for the pictures were few and well chosen, the books such as never grow old, the music lying on the well-worn piano of the sort which is never out of fashion, and standing somewhat apart was one small statue in a recess full of flowers. Lovely in its simple grace and truth was the figure of a child looking upward as if watching the airy flight of some butterfly which had evidently escaped from the chrysalis still lying in the little hand.

Paul was looking at it with approving eyes when Mrs. Dean appeared with his card in her hand, three shawls on her shoulders, and in her face a somewhat startled expression, as if she expected some novel demonstration from the man whose genius her daughter so much admired.

"I hope Miss Psyche is well," began Paul, with great discrimination if not originality.

The delightfully commonplace remark tranquillized Mrs. Dean at once, and, taking off the upper shawl with a fussy gesture, she settled herself for a chat.

"Yes, thank Heaven, Sy is well. I don't know what would become of us if she wasn't It has been a hard and sorrowful year for us with Mr. Dean's business embarrassments, my feeble health, and May's death. I don't know that you were aware of our loss, sir;" and unaffected maternal grief gave sudden dignity to the faded, fretful face of the speaker.

Paul murmured his regrets, understanding better now the pathetic words on a certain tear-stained page of the little book still in his pocket.

"Poor dear, she suffered everything, and it came very hard upon Sy, for the child wasn't happy with any one else, and almost lived in her arms," continued Mrs. Dean, dropping the second shawl to get her handkerchief.

"Miss Psyche has not had much time for art-studies this year, I suppose?" said Paul, hoping to arrest the shower natural as it was.

"How could she, with two invalids, the housekeeping, pa and the boys to attend to? No, she gave that up last spring, and though it was a great disappointment to her at the time, she has got over it now, and is happier than she ever was before, I think," added her mother, remembering as she spoke that Psyche even now went about the house sometimes pale and silent, with a hungry look in her eyes.

' I am glad to hear it," though a little shadow passed over his face as Paul spoke, for he was too true an artist to believe that any work could be as happy as that which he loved and lived for. "I thought there was much promise in Miss Psyche, and I sincerely believe that time will prove me a true prophet," he said with mingled regret and hope in his voice as he glanced about the room, which betrayed the tastes still cherished by the girl.

"I'm afraid ambition isn't good for women; I mean the sort that makes 'em known by coming before the public in any way. But Sy deserves some reward, I'm sure, and I know she'll have it, for a better daughter never lived."

Here the third shawl was cast off, as if the thought of Psyche, or the presence of a genial guest, had touched Mrs. Dean's chilly nature with a comfortable warmth.

Further conversation was interrupted by the avalanche of boys, which came tumbling down the front stairs as Tom, Dick, and Harry shouted in a sort of chorus: —

"Sy, my balloon has got away; lend us a hand at catching him!"

"Sy, I want a lot of paste made, right off."

"Sy, I've split my jacket down the back; come sew me up, there's a dear!"

On beholding a stranger the young gentlemen suddenly lost their voices, found their manners, and with nods and grins took themselves away as quietly as could be expected of six clumping boots and an unlimited quantity of animal spirits in a high state of effervescence. As they trooped off an unmistakable odor of burnt milk pervaded the air, and the crash of china, followed by an Irish wail, caused Mrs. Dean to clap on her three shawls again and excuse herself in visible trepidation.

Paul laughed quietly to himself, then turned sober and said, "Poor Psyche!" with a sympathetic sigh. He roamed about the room impatiently till the sound of voices drew him to the window to behold the girl coming up the walk with her clumsy old father leaning on one arm, the other loaded with baskets and bundles, and her hands occupied by a remarkably ugly turtle.

"Here we are!" cried a cheery voice, as they entered without observing the new-comer. "I've done all my errands and had a lovely time. There is Tom's gunpowder, Dick's fish-hooks, and one of Professor Gazzy's famous turtles for Harry. Here are your bundles, mother dear, and, best of all, here's pa, home in time for a good rest before dinner. I went to the mill and got him."

Psyche spoke as if she had brought a treasure; and so she had, for though Mr. Dean's face usually was about as expressive as the turtle's, it woke and warmed with the affection which his daughter had fostered till no amount of flannel could extinguish it. His big hand patted her cheek very gently as he said, in a tone of fatherly love and pride: —

"My little Sy never forgets old pa, does she?"

"Good gracious me, my dear, there's *such* a mess in the kitchen! Katy's burnt up the pudding, put castor-oil instead of olive in the salad, smashed the best meat-dish, and here's Mr. Gage come to dinner," cried Mrs. Dean in accents of despair as she tied up her head in a fourth shawl.

"Oh, I'm so glad; I'll go in and see him a few

minutes, and then I'll come and attend to everything; so don't worry, mother."

"How did you find me out?" asked Psyche as she shook hands with her guest and stood looking up at him with all the old confiding frankness in her face and manner.

"The violets showed me the way."

She glanced at the posy in his button-hole and smiled.

"Yes, I gave them to Adam, but I didn't think you would guess. I enjoyed your work for an hour to-day, and I have no words strong enough to express my admiration."

"There is no need of any. Tell me about yourself; what have you been doing all this year?" he asked, watching with genuine satisfaction the serene and sunny face before him, for discontent, anxiety, and sadness were no longer visible there.

"I've been working and waiting," she began.

"And succeeding, if I may believe what I see and hear and read," he said with an expressive little wave of the book as he laid it down before her.

"My diary! I didn't know I had lost it. Where did you find it?"

"By the brook where I stopped to rest. The moment I saw your name I shut it up. Forgive me, but I can't ask pardon for reading a few pages of that little gospel of patience, love, and self-denial."

She gave him a reproachful look and hurried the telltale book out of sight as she said, with a momentary shadow on her face:—

"It has been a hard task; but I think I have learned it, and am just beginning to find that my dream *is* 'a noonday light and truth,' to me."

"Then you do not relinquish your hopes and lay down your tools?" he asked with some eagerness.

"Never! I thought at first that I could not serve two masters; but in trying to be faithful to one I find I am nearer and dearer to the other. My cares and duties are growing lighter every day (or I have learned to bear them better), and when my leisure does come I shall know how to use it, for my head is full of ambitious plans, and I feel that I can do something *now*."

All the old enthusiasm shone in her eyes, and a sense of power betrayed itself in voice and gesture as she spoke.

"I believe it," he said heartily. "You have learned the secret, as that proves."

Psyche looked at the childish image as he pointed to it, and into her face there came a motherly expression that made it very sweet.

"That little sister was so dear to me I could not fail to make her lovely, for I put my heart into my work. The year has gone, but I don't regret it, though this is all I have done."

"You forgot your three wishes; I think the year has granted them."

"What were they?"

"To possess beauty in yourself, the power of seeing it in all things, and the art of reproducing it with truth."

She colored deeply under the glance which accompanied the threefold compliment, and answered with grateful humility, —

"You are very kind to say so; I wish I could believe it." Then, as if anxious to forget herself, she added rather abruptly, —

"I hear you think of giving your Adam a mate, — have you begun yet?"

"Yes, my design is finished, all but the face."

"I should think you could image Eve's beauty since you have succeeded so well with Adam's."

"The features perhaps, but not the expression. That is the charm of feminine faces, a charm so subtile that few can catch and keep it. I want a truly womanly face, one that shall be sweet and strong without being either weak or hard. A hopeful, loving, earnest face, with a tender touch of motherliness in it, and perhaps the shadow of a grief that has softened but not saddened it."

"It will be hard to find a face like that."

"I don't expect to find it in perfection; but one sometimes sees faces which suggest all this, and in rare moments give glimpses of a lovely possibility."

"I sincerely hope you will find one then," said Psyche, thinking of the dinner.

"Thank you; *I* think I have."

Now, in order that every one may be suited, we will stop here, and leave our readers to finish the story as they like. Those who prefer the good old fashion may believe that the hero and heroine fell in love, were married and lived bappily ever afterward. But those who can conceive of a world outside of a wedding-ring may believe that the friends remained faithful friends all their lives, while Paul won fame and fortune, and Psyche grew beautiful with the beauty of a serene and sunny nature, happy in duties which became pleasures, rich in the art which made life lovely to herself and others.

www.ingramcontent.com/pod-product-compliance
Lightning Source LLC
Chambersburg PA
CBHW030303170426
43202CB00009B/852